A COURSE IN MIRACLES
A GIFT FOR ALL MANKIND

D0290161

A COURSE IN MIRACLES

A GIFT FOR ALL MANKIND

Tara Singh

LIFE ACTION PRESS
Los Angeles

10 9 8 7 6 5 4 3

Library of Congress Cataloging in Publication Data
Singh, Tara, 1919-
A course in miracles — a gift for all mankind.

1. Foundation for Inner Peace. Course in miracles.
2. Spiritual life. I. Title.
BP610.S5613 1986   299'.93   86-12073
ISBN 1-55531-013-3 Limited Edition, Hardbound
ISBN 1-55531-014-1 Softcover

I am most grateful for the goodness of the following friends for their assistance in the preparation of this book: Charles Johnson, Jim Cheatham, Lucille Frappier, Aliana Scurlock, Clio Dixon, Kris Heagh, Frank Nader, Ted Ward and John Williams.

Contents

Foreword

The oral tradition of teaching is an ancient and honored one. Mr. Singh shares from that tradition. Because of this, in preparing this book we have attempted to retain the cadence, rhythm and flavor of the spoken word rather than to adhere to strict rules of grammar.

The Preface as well as Part II, The Challenge, employ a prose style which might best be described as prose in poetic form. Mr. Singh frequently utilizes this prose style when conveying lofty or serious concepts. The style is particularly appropriate at such times because it gives a weight and spaciousness to the words that could not be so readily achieved otherwise. Whenever such passages occur the reader would benefit greatly by pausing at the end of each line, thus giving greater attention and space to what is being communicated.

Editor

Preface

The impact of one encounter
has the power to bring man to holy relationship
with everyone in the world
because Life is One and Love indivisible.
A single meeting of Andrew, John and Peter with Jesus
transformed their lives for all times
by introducing them to eternity.
A Teacher of God does not
acknowledge separation as real
but only as a mistake which can be corrected.

My very first encounter with *A Course in Miracles*
brought me into direct contact with the vitality
inherent in the Thoughts of God of the Course.
The only reality is the Will of God
which eternally extends itself.
Time is the only illusion.

The pure energy of the Thoughts of God
makes application of the daily lesson
of *A Course in Miracles* possible.
Every single sentence is endowed with the miracle
to undo the illusion of time.
The Holy Spirit awakens the student
from the belief in separation

and accompanies him all through the day.

> *As the teacher of God advances in his training,*
> *he learns one lesson with increasing thorough-*
> *ness. He does not make his own decisions; he*
> *asks his Teacher for His answer, and it is this he*
> *follows as his guide for action.*[1]

Almost all scriptures are written
by those who were inspired by the Incarnations of God.
But *A Course in Miracles* is the direct Thoughts of God.
It is not a religion.
Its purpose is to help the individual find inner peace.

> *This is a course in how to know yourself.*[2]

> *To your most holy Self all praise is due for what*
> *you are, and for what He is Who created you as*
> *you are.*[3]

In an age where:

> *My meaningless thoughts*
> *are showing me a meaningless world,*[4]

a sense of helplessness surrounds man.
Pressured by time and problems,
he is ruled by insecurity and unfulfillment.
Man has already lost his work
and is now subject to a job.
Thus he is false to himself.
Imperceptibly, man everywhere
is reduced to being a mercenary.
Living by mere choices,
he has lost the discrimination and wisdom
to make his own decisions.

Wisdom is one's own; it is direct,
not externally influenced.
Its clarity is what it would take
to see a fact as a fact.

But *A Course in Miracles* comes to awaken him
from manmade illusion
to the God-created Self which realizes:

I am not the victim of the world I see.[5]

The student who makes contact
with the energy of the Course
gives integrity to everything he does.
He starts by bringing order in his life
and lives by:

I will not value what is valueless.[6]

The Course insists that we dissolve
every contradiction and conflict instantly.
This means undoing opinions
and judgments with their consequences
in order to come to Holy Relationship.
Thus the Holy Spirit teaches
the consistency of moving from fact to fact,
until one ends the separation
and comes to the Action of Life itself.

*　*　*　*　*

When I first encountered the Course,
I came to a decision to fully give myself
to discover the truth of its daily lesson.

It led me from understanding the Course intellectually
to making it real —
a recognition of being, untouched by words.
Intellectual understanding is of mere ideas.
A Course in Miracles is to be lived.
Realization is your discovery
that the Thoughts of God are true
and recognition restores the awareness
of your own magnitude and wholeness.

I discovered:

> The curriculum is highly individualized, and all
> aspects are under the Holy Spirit's particular
> care and guidance. Ask and He will answer. The
> responsibility is His, and He alone is fit to
> assume it.

> To do so is His function.
> To refer the questions to Him is yours.[7]

> Prepare for this each morning, remember God
> when you can throughout the day, ask the Holy
> Spirit's help when it is feasible to do so, and
> thank Him for His guidance at night.[8]

As the Course points out,
the function of the Son of God — each one of us —
is to share.
Even though I had resistance to wanting to teach
(because it was my conviction
that one should not interfere in the life of another
unless one knows the truth)
I was brought to the awareness of the eternal laws
of the teaching-learning relationship
that the Manual for Teachers points out:

*The course . . . emphasizes that to teach is to
learn. . . . It also emphasizes that teaching is a
constant process. . . .*[9]

*In the teaching-learning situation, each one
learns that giving and receiving are the same.*[10]

Therefore I realized that
the Name of God cannot be commercialized.
Obviously love energizes itself by sharing.
How can the Given be sold?
Love is not of past or future.
What is of the living moment is the sharing of

. . . everlasting holiness and peace.[11]

The one-to-one relationship leads to the
meeting in the Oneness of Life where separation ends.

In 1983, the One Year Non-Commercialized Retreat:
A Serious Study of *A Course in Miracles* began
with students from all over the country.
Bringing *A Course in Miracles* into application
changed our lifestyle and values.
We discovered the need
of being independent of the externals through:

Self reliance
Intrinsic work
and
Having something of one's own to give.

Freed from a sense of lack,
a small group of men and women
have stepped out of jobs and live a productive life.

Do you realize what is involved
in coming to self reliance?
Would you consider
who would work with a small group
and give himself to a non-commercialized life?
Would it not have to be an action born of fulfillment?

Without the vitality of gratefulness no one can overcome the self-centered outlook of commercial life. You and I would have to be related to the given strength of the One Who is . . . *in charge of the process of Atonement* .[12] In the *Text,* the Author of *A Course in Miracles,* the Son of God, speaks in the first person:

> *I am in charge of the process of Atonement, which I undertook to begin. When you offer a miracle to any of my brothers, you do it to your-self and me. . . . My part in the Atonement is the cancelling out of all errors that you could not otherwise correct. When you have been restored to the recognition of your original state, you naturally become part of the Atonement your-self. As you share my unwillingness to accept er-ror in yourself and others, you must join the great crusade to correct it; listen to my voice, learn to undo error and act to correct it.*[13]

We have completed three years of the one-to-one relationship under the auspices of the Foundation for Life Action, a federally approved, nonprofit educa-tional foundation.

From this intensive study
of the curriculum of *A Course in Miracles*
there now emerges a School —
"Having the Ears to Hear" —

situated at *The Branching of the Road*.[14]
The School deals with
MAN'S INHERENT UNWILLINGNESS
to change from passive to co-creative energies.
Its curriculum is consistent with *A Course in Miracles*.
It is for the serious student
whose first love is God,
for whom nothing short of ending the separation
is acceptable.
The School is not for those who want to be the student
but for those who are already the student and:

"... have the ears to hear."[15]

The *Text* states:

> *When you come to the place where the branch in the road is quite apparent, you cannot go ahead. You must go either one way or the other. . . . The whole purpose of coming this far was to decide which branch you will take now. The way you came no longer matters. It can no longer serve. No one who reaches this far can make the wrong decision, although he can delay.*[16]

The Foundation for Life Action
is not just an organization.
It has become a school for training teachers
to bring *A Course in Miracles* into application
in order to be part of God's Plan for Salvation.
It provides an atmosphere
in which to live a lifestyle
consistent with the Path of Virtue.
We do not seek donations or ask for charity;
nor do we have a community or own any property.

In order for the student to be non-dependent on externals, and overcome insecurity and self-centeredness, we undertake:

— Not to work for another.
— To discover our own intrinsic work.
— To be self reliant.
— To have something of our own to give.
— To lead a non-commercialized life.
    and
— Not to take advantage of another.

> *The teachers of God have trust in the world, because they have learned that it is not governed by the laws the world made up. It is governed by a Power That is in them but not of them. It is this Power That keeps all things safe. It is through this Power that the teachers of God look on a forgiven world.*[17]

For us the fact is:

> *Only God's plan for salvation will work.*[18]

> *My only function is the one God gave me.*[19]

> *A happy outcome to all things is sure.*[20]

> *No one can fail who seeks to reach the truth.*[21]

* * * * *

This book, *A Course in Miracles — A Gift for All Mankind* is drawn from the sharings which have taken place during the three years since the beginning of the One Year Non-Commercialized Retreat.

Tara Singh

Introduction

I often feel that without *A Course in Miracles* my life would have been empty. One such gift makes everything possible, makes life meaningful. Who brought it? How did it ever come to the earth plane? It just leaves one with wonder.

Why was *A Course in Miracles* given when there are already so many religions and scriptures in the world? And all scriptures are holy regardless of which religion's they are part of. The words of the Hebrew prophets are true; the words of great Chinese sages are Absolute Knowledge; the words of Indian saints are eternal and true. So, also, the words of Islam, the Koran, are of God. Why then another book?

Why did *A Course in Miracles* come today? Why in our generation? Why in English? Why was man deprived of it for twenty centuries, fifty centuries?

What answers would you give to these questions? If you give answers born out of relative knowledge they are not answers at all.

We are so educated. We know so much that it is very difficult to receive a truth. Our very knowing has become one of the most detrimental things in life.

If you are sensitive and sincere, you must feel the pain of not knowing reality, of not knowing love or truth directly. Do you ever feel that? Have you ever yearned for truth? If you have you won't settle for the false.

PART I

1   *Why A Course In Miracles?*

In order to see what brought *A Course in Miracles* into being, we have to look at what necessitated it.

There is an Eternal Law that a need must be met. So the Course is not something whimsical that somebody just wrote. It is the gift of God to His Son. We have to see the importance of it. When you approach that which is boundless, you go to it with reverence — receptive and quiet — not with knowing.

Somewhere, deep within each one of us, there must have been a tremendous cry for something beyond what was already in the scriptures — to have something that was direct, that could be understood. Most of the scriptures of the world have been translated and interpreted. And when interpretation takes place, the human thought that is of relative knowledge interferes with it.

NOTE: *A Course in Miracles* consists of three volumes: *Text, Workbook for Students* and *Manual for Teachers*. The *Text* sets forth the concepts on which the thought system of the Course is based. The *Workbook for Students*, three hundred and sixty-five lessons, is designed to make possible the application of the concepts presented in the *Text*. The *Manual for Teachers* provides answers to some of the basic questions a student of the Course might ask and defines many of the terms used in the *Text*.(Editor)

And yet there is a yearning in each one of us to know God, to know truth, to know peace, to know love — all that which is not accessible to the conscious mind. We substitute attachment for love, opinion and belief for truth, pleasure for joy. And hardly anyone has gone beyond these substitutes. Each person thinks that he loves, that he knows the truth. We are so convinced about our opinions and our feelings — even about our limitations.

But we are saying that beyond our opinions and feelings there is a yearning in us to know the truth, to know the real, to know the timelessness of our being. This yearning has led us throughout the ages. Before Buddha, before Jesus, before Moses, before Mohammed — this yearning was there.

The yearning comes when I separate myself from God. That is the only state I've known throughout my life. Separation. That's why there is the yearning for wholeness and holiness. If I am whole, all things are solved; all is resolved. Separation must always have need for peace, for wholeness, for contentment. As long as separation is there, the yearning is there.

It is this yearning within each one of us that has brought about *A Course in Miracles*.

No scripture of this kind has ever come. It is in English — the most evolved English you will encounter anywhere. By that I mean it is precise, exact. It defines every word. It is not vague and it does not use one single word that is not a fact. Therefore, it doesn't preach; it just presents the fact.

A Course in Miracles relates to man directly. It deals with the issues we have to face within ourselves. This is the one thing that mankind has consistently avoided throughout the centuries. We can always read about the lives of others. But we don't need Moses to come and part the sea again.

Because the Course deals with our issues and not the past, we have to undo the past. This clarity — this Absolute Knowledge of God — can only be received if we are in the present. When we are in the present, then we are true to ourselves and can receive that which is Absolute. Then we are free from all our knowings because the past cannot enter. When the past cannot enter, you are the light unto yourself. And it is this state that can be called religious.

For when you are in the present, whatever anyone has said in the past is no longer applicable. When Jesus said, "I and my Father are one,"[1] it was His truth at that time, not yours when you say it. If you say, "I and my Father are one," isn't it a lie? It is just words, and limited to the brain.

We need to understand what the human brain is and what it does. The human brain is physical. It has a record of all that has happened to an individual, all he has experienced and learned. It is the storehouse. It does not know anything other than what has been put into it. So, he is limited to what he has known.

That's called the human brain. It functions like the computer — what is put into it comes out. As a matter of fact, the human being is now a second rate computer, reduced to nothing but jobs. It's tragic.

We are laying a foundation so you can really become aware of a yearning within for *A Course in Miracles*, a direct word of God. Can we come to that intensity, so you become aware you want to be out of this mess of knowings that have been prejudiced; that you want to be reborn, become alive, resurrected; that you want to know the Absolute — not opinions but the Absolute. Love is Absolute. The brain can't know it, and the computer can't know it.

You, as an individual, have the responsibility to be wise and not be misled. You are a child of God, a creation of clarity. Don't ever underestimate your potential. The systems have always fallen apart. Whether it's the Roman or the Greek or the British — systems have never succeeded. Napoleons have come and gone and the Hitlers and the Czars. They don't last. But the human being does.

The wise never loses confidence in the human being and he never trusts a system. It doesn't matter by what name the system goes — in the end they are all corrupted. That is the effect of time on things — it corrodes everything, brings it down and corrupts it. Even if it starts out right, give it time, it will start deteriorating. Everywhere it is the same.

Today it is helplessness that mankind worships. And there is nothing religious about helplessness. Tell me who is not helpless and dependent on someone else. Where there's dependence there is no relationship. Relationship is at the level of life itself, not at the level of concepts and ideas.

To give importance to systems, to dogmas, and to ideologies is to ignore your own importance. You are far beyond and bigger than these. You are eternal and they are not. When men deceive men to believe in a system, you can see the beginning of the end of that system. At the age of nineteen, Ralph Waldo Emerson, seeing the invention of the locomotive, said that the seeds of destruction are inherent in this progress. Are we capable of heeding or are we going to continue promoting so-called progress?

Lincoln has warned us. He said that prosperity breeds tyrants. Are we capable of hearing? It would revolutionize our lives. We have to find the wisdom to get out of the mess we're in. We are drugged and still go on.

Where is our independence? Where is our individuality? No one is really individual because we are all ruled by fear and insecurity.We have but one brain and we are all subject to its conditioning. Fear is not Chinese. Nor is anger Indian. Nor is insecurity American. Even though they are manmade. Once you have fear, whether you are Indian or Chinese or American, you act the same way.

To be an individual you have to be free of fear. You have to have a different outlook on life. How can you say you're an individual when you are a victim of fear and insecurity and anger and greed and jealousies and all the rest? We have been deceived. It's time we wake up! But can we afford it? It requires wisdom.

Wisdom is rare. It takes guts. It demands a sense of dignity, responsibility. Wisdom has the ability to say ''no,'' the ability not to react. Wisdom is your own love, your own awakening. It flowers in you. When you are with wisdom you know that you're holy. And the holy do not scare the world. They don't organize anything or promote a belief system. They become humane, and their light cannot be hidden. What they do is ever new because it is an extension of the Source of Life, not separated from Life.

When you are not related, then you are isolated. Then you need jobs to support yourself and all kinds of sensation to live with yourself — beer, cigarettes, television, magazines. Everything. To forget yourself. Just to somehow never face yourself. Constant restlessness.

Over the centuries man had the notion that if he was not poor, then he would be happy. And today we have affluence and with it more psychosomatic diseases, more rapes, more murders, more suicides, than any other time we have known. Where have marriages gone? Where has the reverence of children for parents gone? And we still keep on believing in our illusions?

We thought if we got educated, that would improve our lot: maybe the whole misery of life was because we lacked education. So man got educated. But still there is no wisdom. We became affluent, there's still no wisdom. Education and affluence have become a means to further deterioration. Can you see that? More wars, more hate, more propaganda, more restlessness, more distraction. Distractions. Distractions. Distractions.

Life has become an indulgence: working like a machine from nine to five for somebody else; reduced to nothing but a life of habit and routine. And we are planning, full blast, head-on, universal destruction. That's a fact. Education without wisdom is self-destructive.

There is a manmade world and a God created world. We live in a manmade world. The God created world requires wisdom. It doesn't matter if you're a philosopher or a peasant. It takes wisdom to know the God created world. When you're related with that, you harness the energy of it, the wisdom of it. You also know your own dignity, your own sacredness. Now you know your skills, your insecurity, and your fear of losing a job.

Then we thought, ''Well, maybe the religions will help.'' The religions haven't helped either — neither the Kabala, nor the yoga, the Gita, nor the Bible. Because we thought by learning. . . Well, tell me what have you learned? Can you learn wisdom? Can you learn to be free of fear? You can read about Moses all you want, about Elijah or Daniel. You can read the Koran and you can read the Vedas, but your reading is merely an activity of the brain. You can memorize them; you can quote them; become a professor, a priest. And you'll be nothing but a professional in the end.

A saint is not a professional. He's never in the shrines where man has been indoctrinated with one ''ism'' after another. How could he live in a world of fragmentation?

Could you be a saint and be a Christian? Could you be a saint and still be a Hindu? Could you be a saint and remain a Moslem? You are grateful that it served its purpose. You're out of it. You have become universal. Then you free man from his prejudices, from his conflicts. You talk about wholeness because you have come to wholeness.

So, the religions have not helped, affluence has

not helped, education has not helped. And all the political dogmas have not helped either. Man is more bound than ever before.

But now, after centuries, a miracle has happened. A real miracle. And somehow, can you imagine, we can't even recognize a miracle anymore. We're so fatigued and tired by the routine. We're so educated — to the teeth — that we've lost innocence! We've lost silence! We have no knowing of stillness within. Our so-called knowing has become our bondage. And it doesn't know reality. It knows the names of stars, metals, trees and animals, but it doesn't know life.

So then the miracle happened. *A Course in Miracles* came. It says the learning has not worked, neither religion, nor affluence — none of these things have worked. Why? Because the only thing that will work is if learning is brought into application — that what is lacking is application.

So the politician can speak *about* something, but nobody applies it. They're talking about peace and preparing for war. Tell me which one isn't. He wouldn't be in the game. No one would nominate Lincoln today. He would refuse to get his beard trimmed and shoes polished and put on the clothes that Madison Avenue tells him to. He would be a man of conviction who doesn't compromise, who has a voice. And no one would listen to him.

A man like Lincoln would start undoing your illusions. Wouldn't he? In order to help, he would start undoing — making some space — to free you from the bind. But you don't want to let go of your belief systems. And that's true everywhere. I'm not talking about a particular country or people. I'm talking about everywhere in the world. I'm talking about man — the human being. How he's been indoctrinated, whether in Chile or China or India. It doesn't matter where. Unless you're part of the clan, you're in trouble.

And the masses just go along because they have no mind of their own. To have a mind you have to have wisdom. Then you don't fit into it. You have your own resources and what you do is new. Then you'll appreciate *A Course in Miracles* because it starts with the undoing. It doesn't promote anything.

A Course in Miracles tells us the truth. And one wonders why, after all these thousands and thousands of years, that it had to be the Course that would tell us the truth. Have you ever thought about that? You can read the Bible, the Talmud, the Koran, and the Shastras. They are very inspiring and they're very true but it's the Course that tells us the truth as we would understand it.

Prophets after prophets have come to the world. They did great things and we worshipped them, gave them our reverence and respect. But it was always they who did it, so to speak. The rest of us got lost again in seeking gratification and security, caught in our prejudices and the activity of the physical senses.

A Course in Miracles gives *us* the keys to overcome the world. It has no symbology. This is phenomenal. This was the next step that had to be taken. He Who overcame the world had to find ways to help us do the same. It is like holding the brother by the hand and leading him to freedom from the world.

What a blessed generation we are. This took place in our time and how little we know. In all our eons of life, we took birth this time to be amongst the blessed generation that was to know the truth. If we have the ears to hear.

It is a wonder that such a thing could exist. How much we deprive ourselves when we lack discrimination and appreciation. It's like some kind of paralysis that just can't soar with appreciation — so alien to gratefulness are we.

A Course in Miracles is anonymous. Someone gave us the Course. That someone rose to the *state* of the Course — surpassed the nameless names, became One, and therefore never wrote their name on it, never said, ''It's me.''

It's very interesting that out of probably the most materialistic country in the world emerges the greatest gift ever given to humanity. It defies all laws, all assumptions, all judgments. It's like Moses freeing the slaves, and Guru Nanak taking the untouchables out of misery, and the Course, liberating us from materialistic mentality.

For a long time hardly anyone recognized Jesus. To recognize, to realize the greatness of Jesus in his own time would have taken a tremendous sense of discrimination. To recognize that which is eternal demands wisdom, eyes that see. And therefore, hardly anyone recognized Jesus for who He was. Appearance is deceptive.

A Course in Miracles has come to the New World to bring it to new consciousness. And it offers application. It helps us with the application. It says never mind the belief system — whether you are Buddhist, Christian, Hindu, whatever you are. It doesn't matter. You can read the Course because miracles are not belief systems. A miracle is only the relationship of the body with that which is not of the body. The correction has to take place within you, not in the synagogue or in the church or at a temple. You are the temple of God, because that is where the transformation takes place.

Religions have become organized and preach their dogmas. The Buddhists teach Buddhism. Don't they? Some ritual, some form, some procedure. And Hinduism and Christianity and so forth do the same. But they haven't brought about application, they have merely spread their own belief systems. The Christian missionaries go out and the Islamic missionaries go out. You don't know how much they are a part of the wars that have pursued them.

When you convert, finally, you end up facing that force. You understand? They clash. In converting people, you do not relate them to the Source, you just relate them to your belief system. And belief systems are of the brain, of the earth. That which is not of the earth is given to you when you are still and therefore, part of God's Mind. Without stillness you will never know that which is eternal, that which is real. There is less and less stillness in the world and more and more haste and pressure.

So *A Course in Miracles* came saying that we don't have to be dependent upon another mortal or another system. It begins with you. And you won't believe this, but that's not what we really want. We want to deal with people out there. We'll do anything to evade confronting ourselves.

There are two kinds of teachers. One promotes the preaching of the dogma — the Buddhists are so happy, they are talking about Nirvana; and Christians are happy talking about the Kingdom of God. The Hindus have their Gods, and the Moslems say there is the holy prophet Mohammed. Each religion has that. They externalize. But in order to externalize you have to use the brain because to the Mind of God, nothing is external.

To the enlightened being nothing is external. That's why he can look at the tree and see the eternal, purifying vitality of water and air. Being one with the Mind of God, which does not externalize, he sees the fallacy in which man is caught. Don't you see? And he tries to restore it, saying "Look! You are eternal." But he doesn't say it's Buddhist, or Hindu. He just says you're it.

So, in *A Course in Miracles* it is you who become important. For you are no less than any prophet that ever lived. You are as much a part of the Mind of God as the so-called prophet. The only thing is that the prophet realized that truth. You see? And he tried to share it with others, telling them, "You can do it."

"You can do what I have done, and more."[2]

And there is a great need in the world for us to know that. Then our sharing would become automatic. You would start extending the wholeness, because that is what you are. Otherwise, you'll extend some belief system — whether it's Christian or Hindu, political or economic.

What is it you are extending? If you're confused, you're going to elect a confused president. Confusion must project confusion. Confused people elect confused prime ministers.

It's so childish and simple. Why do you have to belong to this mania? Why don't you find your own reality, your own resources?

Where do you think *A Course in Miracles* would start? What would be the starting point of the Mind of God? Where? It must start with undoing. It would have to.

We talked about the two kinds of teachers. One extends the belief system that supports him. He doesn't believe *I am sustained by the Love of God.*[3] He knows he is sustained by his church. So that's what he is going to promote. I could be very successful extending Hinduism, even with all its untouchability. I can say nice things about karma and reincarnation and you'll think, "Christianity doesn't have that. This sounds great!" Can we stop? Can you discover your own self? That would require some stillness, wouldn't it?

A Course in Miracles doesn't have anything to sell. It's not a belief system. The Course is the Thoughts of God. When it says, *I am sustained by the Love of God,* that's the truth. If you realize the truth of it, then you know it. If you merely want to know it intellectually, it doesn't do a thing. So the responsibility is yours and mine.

The Course would have to start — the Thoughts of God would have to start — with undoing. Undoing is to question the deceptions into which we have fallen. Is that word understood now? Undoing. Not more learning, but unlearning. To question our learning.

Why would the Course start that way and why does a real teacher start that way? That's a wonderful question, isn't it? Why does the real teacher, why does the Thought of God, why does *A Course in Miracles* start with undoing, saying look at the deceptions? Why? Because, the Real is the only One that has realized the truth — that you are already perfect.

Anyone who has realized the truth that you are already perfect is not going to sell perfection or what you have to do to get there. He's going to say, "Look, the layers and layers of conditioning that blind you to the light are what you have to remove." And the other one who comes and sells belief systems knows nothing of the fact that the human being is perfect.

So the Course starts with undoing. How does it undo? The first lesson is *Nothing I see . . . means anything.*[4] That's quite a blow. Unless you come to humility about it, you're at war. You think you know everything; it's saying you don't.

The next lesson is, *I have given everything I see . . . all the meaning that it has for me.*[5] And that's true too. When I buy a chair I protect it, hold on to it, and call the police if I see you take it. So I'm giving it meaning. But ideas have no meaning. The knowing of the manmade thought system is no knowing at all. Just like the word chair doesn't mean anything — it's a name given to a symbol — so are ideas abstract. Among ideas, this is good and that is bad, because they are based on duality. The Course doesn't go into duality. Duality is *our* conflict.

It's like the two Zen monks. They were to cross a stream and they saw a young lady who couldn't make it across. And one of them put her on his back and carried her across the stream. After awhile, the other one scolded, "I can't understand. You're never to look at a woman. You're never to touch one. What did you do? How could you do it? You're a monk!" And the other one said, "Well, I left her there. You're still carrying her."

A Course in Miracles brings us to the sanity that begins to question. And by questioning our belief system, we can dissolve it. It is the Thought of God because the Thought of God can dissolve manmade thought. And when it dissolves the manmade thought, you are free.

The only freedom, like Thoreau said, is freedom from self. When I'm responsible for myself in the true sense, then I'm free from my brain activity and "earth energy," with all its aggression and survival instinct. When I'm free of that, then I am at peace — in that state of stillness. Then you want nothing, for you are not of the earth, you are of the Kingdom of God. And you have nothing to preach. You introduce your brothers to eternity; and you don't charge for it because you have overcome insecurity. You are not part of the survival system of man that leads to greed and cleverness and a routine life.

You are a free person, full of gratefulness in your heart for the glory of creation. Even the earth creates the most beautiful flowers in its joy of being. Everything sings the glory of God in creation, never wanting to be anything other than what it is. A tree is a tree, a fruit is a fruit. There is perfection in the orange. There is perfection in the seed of the orange that can again produce endless oranges, and in the juice, the color. The color. Who knows the reality of the color? You could heal just by looking at the color itself if you knew what a color was.

We look at the world with sightless eyes because we are preoccupied with the brain and thought. It's time that we opened our eyes. Eyes of the still mind see the miracle that the tree is, the miracle that the child is — see perfection in everything.

The manifest world can relate you to that which is perfect, but you have to see it with stillness. The purpose of everything that is manifested is to relate you with its source. And the source is eternal, all encompassing. A flower did not come about without the moon; without the moon it could not have grown. Without the sun, the soil, the air, without the water, without the light, it could not have grown. It relates you to everything in existence. The brain separates everything. The brain takes everything away from the wholeness and fragments it. The action of God's Thought is to bring it back to wholeness.

A Course in Miracles starts with undoing. It questions our belief systems and it even questions our understanding. Yet, its approach is compassionate. The Course points out that even if you don't believe in it, or you don't quite understand it, it's quite alright — just do the simple exercises and don't make a problem out of it. As you go along you begin to see these simple lessons making a change which is quite involuntary. There is probably more to it than we realize. Every scripture has a certain vitality of its own.

After we have done about ten lessons, we see some of them repeated in a slightly different form. It is like a spiral. *A Course in Miracles* points out that it is a process of Atonement. Atonement is a word — a religious word — to which some people have a reaction. It simply means the ending of separation. The Course is a process of ending the separation. And when the same lesson, more or less, reappears we seem to understand it a little better. It makes a lot more sense than when we first saw it.

These thoughts do not mean anything [6] appears the second time as *My thoughts do not mean anything.*[7] If you could say *My thoughts do not mean anything* with honesty, you would be enlightened.

Now we can see that we say all kinds of things, can utter the words and even say that we understand them — that we agree with them — but it doesn't really mean very much. That which is true has to be lived. We begin to see in a very gentle way that the problem does not lie in coming to the understanding about things. We can understand a great deal. In fact, man's problem today is not that he doesn't know enough but that he knows too much. And his understanding is not always valid. There is a tremendous gap between understanding and application; and it takes wholeheartedness in order to bridge that gap.

Most of the religions of the world have inspired man to live consistent with Divine Laws or with the path of virtue. And each one more or less states the same thing: Love your neighbor, be truthful, know thyself, and so forth. *A Course in Miracles* doesn't leave it at that, having seen that we can repeat the words and still not live them. The Course emphasizes that it has to be lived. Application is essential. For instance, one of the lessons is, *There is nothing to fear.*[8] Now we can all agree with it, we can all even say we read it, but if the fear is still there then we have not.

It becomes very challenging and very confronting. And one way or another we do justify our not bringing it to application. We either say we are tired, we wish the circumstances were different, we would like to do it — all kinds of things. There are very, very few who have brought it to application. Very few who can truthfully say, *There is nothing to fear* or say anything that they really mean. This is quite alarming — that we say things we don't mean.

I am sustained by the Love of God.[9] If you could say it and mean it and not just intellectually understand it, then there is no room for insecurity. It would alter one's life, values, relationship with another, relationship with everything.

One begins to see then the wisdom of the Course for it begins with the undoing of our knowings that know no reality at all. Thought does not relate man to reality. And it is we who give it authority over us.

One of the most wonderful things about *A Course in Miracles* is that it does not preach. This is something! The clergy of the world, for the most part, has done nothing more than preach concepts and beliefs, words and thoughts. If it was ever brought into application, would there be wars in the world? We are quite at ease and comfortable with these inconsistencies in life.

Christianity, like Buddhism or Hinduism and other religions, states that THOU SHALL NOT KILL.[10] And the clergy on all sides have overlooked this. Mere verbal understanding has no meaning. Understanding is that which is lived, brought into application.

The Course doesn't preach, in fact it doesn't even teach if you look very keenly at it. Teaching would again be verbal, would it not? What does one teach but ideas and concepts? And most of us have never questioned if one can teach. We've just taken for granted that somebody else can teach me something. Of course, you can teach someone a skill, but we are talking about reality. Someone can tell you how to peel a potato. But to undo the psychological fears that we project and the concepts that lead us to clash with one another is another matter. If the conflict continues within man then war and discord are only an external manifestation of that conflict within.

The Course has nothing to teach because it doesn't promote dependence. The teachings that say I know and you don't, or the priest knows and the follower doesn't, or some politician knows and you don't, are to be questioned. If they are not at peace within and you are not at peace within, we all meet on the same level.

A man who is at peace is not an ambitious person. We can hardly even imagine what he would be like, what his function in society would be. Probably one thing is sure, that he would be very quickly put in jail. Or he won't get a visa to get in the country. Jesus would have a tough time. He would try to remind us that we say IN GOD WE TRUST. Who trusts in God? And yet we can have that phrase going around for centuries.

When we begin our sessions at the Foundation we

usually sit quietly, often about fifteen minutes. And these fifteen minutes are very intense. One begins to see the vitality of silence; you sense it directly. And this you can also do wherever you are, if the inner chatter, the pressure of time, and the conflict within would allow you. There are two things in this world we can't afford, and one of them is silence. We have too much to do; we are so wound up. The other is innocence. Silence brings man to innocence. Perhaps now we can begin to understand *A Course in Miracles* — it doesn't teach, but brings one to silence, to innocence. That is why it is called *A Course in Miracles.*

Reading the Course — at every paragraph, every sentence — brings illusions to truth and dissolves them. And a miracle takes place. Please try to come to that state where the miracle takes place. We will have to totally change our approach to reading and there are very few people in the world who know to read.

Reading means silencing the mind, not accumulating knowledge. We don't have the right relationship with the Course if we are accumulating more ideas, more beliefs, more knowledge. It must bring one to silence at every sentence and then at the end you are in a different space. There is vitality within you that you never felt before. The strongest experience man can ever have on this planet is the vitality of silence.

Silence is not touched by words; silence is a state where contradictions end and a renewal takes place. There is nothing mysterious nor oriental about it. It doesn't have any means to it, no techniques to it, no secrets to it, no mantras to it. For what has a method brings in the preoccupation of thought again. Whatever busies the mind is in contradiction with innocence and silence and dissipates energy.

So every sentence of *A Course in Miracles* offers the gift of silence and space in which something within each one of us comes to wholeness. It is what you directly experience. It's not someone telling you externally. And that's wonderful. Your own direct experience would change the quality of your reading the Course. Then when you say, *I am sustained by the Love of God,* you would insist that these words be true.

We thought we could live in the world without integrity, without conviction, and the conflict goes on. As long as it goes on, the need for outlets becomes inevitable. Life becomes more and more artificial. And today man is faced with the problem of jobs and unemployment. To the industrial economy, the human being is not important anymore — nuclear submarines are. People can be starving and we don't have the money to feed them, but to send armaments we do. All over the world there is this insanity, this madness for more armament. Many millions of dollars are being spent on armament every hour by the human race and there is starvation, deprivation. It's the opposite of love.

As you read the Course you begin to see that life is eternal, its laws are eternal. Life is sustained by eternal laws. It's been raining for millenia; the sun shines every day. The forest survives after millions of years. It has its own vitality because life is consistent with eternal laws. It has its own rhythm, its own beauty. The planets, the seasons, everything is related. Nothing is outside of it. Life is one.

And man, in his isolation, in his separation, creates

conflict within which results in exploitation of man. All over the world the rich are getting richer, and our value system is becoming more and more corrupt.

So the Course begins to relate us with our eternity. We said earlier that the Course does not preach or teach because it stands on the premise that man is already perfect. We have such difficulty in believing that. In fact, we have difficulty in trusting that our thoughts don't mean anything. We think, ''My God, they do!'' *My meaningless thoughts are showing me a meaningless world*[11] seems so challenging. You get shocked and don't like it but then you begin to see the truth of it.

A Course in Miracles questions our conclusions, our assumptions and opinions in which we are caught — the bondage of our knowings. To free man from his concepts and his beliefs is the Action of Love. What else is there? If you are already perfect, then all you need to know is who you are.

The Course then takes another step — it awakens you and brings you to your own identity. Something is happening in you and you may not even know it. You begin to see, ''My God, this is fantastic! And the Course is not teaching. It's making me aware.'' Because the action of the Course is the Action of Love. It is not thought born, it is not earth born. It doesn't influence because it's an action of the awakening of Love. Love is independent and It must therefore provide independence.

When most people teach, they want you to conform to their belief system. It gives them great comfort; they get the attention. But their teaching cannot be without motive. The thought system of man never functions without motive because it is always unfulfilled. Only in Love is there not the unfulfillment. Love alone is independent because Love alone is of God.

A Course in Miracles has no vested interest. It relates you with your own Identity — not just with Moses, or with Jesus or Buddha, or America or this or that. You're stepping out of the world because you're not of the world. And you're outgrowing everything that is born of time. The thought system of man is of time. All our thinking is of time. And somehow just the touch of awareness that we are eternal takes away the pressures.

And it cannot be done through preaching — only through awakening.

> *If it helps you, think of me holding your hand and leading you. And I assure you this will be no idle fantasy.*[12]

These are the words of Christ. And that promise is met in every single day's lesson. Each lesson is consecrated and blessed.

Your attitudes begin to change. You gain strength and confidence and faith. The Course speaks to the individual: you can still make it.The system can't make it but you can. What a gift of God! To each one — you can make it.

The Course imparts the Divine Laws we have to understand to come to peace and to stillness. In the introduction to the *Text*, it says the only choice you and I have is *when* we want to learn them. But this is the curriculum. It does not promote dogma. It talks about eternal laws that we have lost sight of. For we have gotten caught in ideas. The Course introduces us to our own sacredness. And without sacredness, this world is in chaos.

A Course in Miracles encompasses all religions. Nothing is outside of it, any more than anything is outside of you. It ends fragmentation and the duality between you and God. It says that God's Will is your will. It is God's gift to His Son, and it tells you the truth. It is not concepts. It is not theories. It is not ideas. And when you begin to discover that, you fall in love with the words of truth. Just to hear those words changes us. Just by hearing one is transformed.

So, read it with your heart. It's just a lesson a day. Read the lesson in the morning. Then bring to your remembrance that which is your own Reality. Remembrance doesn't mean that you just think of the lesson every hour. What it really means is that you are declaring your freedom from time, from external pressures, and from the world of illusion and unreality, because you dare to remember that you are eternal.

Then you can say, *Peace to my mind.* . . .[13] And time can't touch it. Time cannot touch peace. No circumstances can invade upon, *Let all my thoughts be still.*[14] Nothing can invade stillness. And this is something already inherent in us. We need to discover that which is eternal.

Just as there is contact in the morning with the Course that revives the remembrance for the day, before going to bed sit quietly, peacefully, come to stillness, and read the *Text*. And within one year, you will find your function. For you will no longer be threatened by what is unreal. Having discovered your reality, that is what you will extend. And you won't make causes; you do not have to belong to anything. You become the light. You become part of that which is Universal. A liberated being brings salvation to all man. And we all have that potential.

So, wherever you are, whatever you are doing, start to make a little space. And as you begin to awaken your own potentials, the external circumstances will change. By themselves. Your own wisdom will know what is right.

And anytime you are pressured you can say, *Peace to my mind. Let all my thoughts be still.* Once they are still, there are no problems because the energy of stillness burns what is unreal. It is like a light that dissolves the darkness — dispels it. A still mind is the Mind of God. It's absolutely independent of the opposite. Then it is at peace. And a man at peace in a troubled world is very much needed.

Could we make a start that way? Then our likes and dislikes are finished. Any problems? How can there be problems in Life? Any questions? It's the same thing. Peace and stillness know no problems, have no questions, and accept no answers. For they are free — of ideas.

2 Approaching Truth
How To Read
A Course In Miracles

What preparation would you go through, my friends, to communicate with the Thought of God? What sincerity, what purity would you bring to your own self, to your own state? With what reverence would you approach It? What attitude? So that you come to a totally different state of being, a humility that can say, ''I have come to receive.'' Humility is what? Putting away your own thought system, putting the ''me and mine'' away. Isn't that so? And then you are almost in meditation just because you're approaching the Thought of God.

Your peace surrounds me, Father. Where I go, Your peace goes there with me. It sheds its light on everyone I meet. I bring it to the desolate and lonely and afraid. I give Your peace to those who suffer pain, or grieve for loss, or think they are bereft of hope and happiness. Send them to me, my Father. Let me bring Your peace with me. For I would save Your Son, as is Your Will, that I may come to recognize my Self.

And so we go in peace. To all the world we give the message that we have received. And thus we come to hear the Voice for God, Who speaks to us as we relate His Word; Whose Love we recognize because we share the Word that He has given unto us.[15]

*   *   *   *   *

Let's talk about *A Course in Miracles* and about reading the books. One of the *Workbook* lessons says:

I love You, Father, and I love Your Son.[16]

And we all think we know what this means. But do we? Honesty is required to know the truth. I suppose a five or six year old child could be taught to read it; and a five or six year old child could also say "I love you," and "I love my doggy," and so on.

As long as we are content with just words — and most of us are — we will never get to know what it really means. And why is it that for so long we have not questioned? We use the word "love" so frequently, but we have hardly any notion of what it really is. I mean the actuality of it. The actual state of love.

Every single knowing is external to it. Every single word — including the word "love" — is external to the actual state of love. That is what love is. It's uncontaminated by words, and it renews itself all the time, every split second.

Every split second all the planets are rotating. You know, the energy? Can you conceive? How many billions of breaths are being taken every second? Can you see the energy behind it? That is what Love is. That kind of energy. Its first impact dissolves all the words and brings one to innocence, to the purity of a saint. And probably he has the right to use that word and no one else has.

So as long as we're going to keep using words without knowing the reality behind the words, we're never going to know what *A Course in Miracles* is saying.

Our reading is not reading at all.

We have over the centuries learned to learn more. This mania of ever wanting more is what regulates our life. Always wanting more and more. Whether it's things, whether it's friends, whether it's properties, whether it's so-called knowledge. Every single thing — we want more of it. And we are becoming the victims of ''more-ness.''

But that's the function of the brain! That would be the first thing love would discover. The brain is hungry for more-ness to keep its preoccupation going. It even pretends to talk about love without knowing it. It's the love of illusion. It's not real. It's the love of words. It's just phraseology.

We cannot read *A Course in Miracles* as long as we are caught in ideas, because the Course is not an idea. It is not abstract. It does not talk about theories. It talks about the actuality of that state — words uttered from that actuality, from that State. And the purpose of the words uttered from that State is to bring you and me to It.

The man of God comes to stillness — to a still mind — because he has seen through the deceptions of thought. And one of the deceptions he sees is that he can never learn. This is going to shock you a little bit. The first thing that stillness discovers is that man can't learn — that the so-called learning is just his mania for self-improvement. Man is already perfect, but he thinks he's not. And therefore, all his learning is an indulgence. And we don't like having that taken away. We have become addicted to the preoccupation of more-ness.

This function of brain activity, the computer-brain, is the first thing the man of God discovers. What a startling fact. The realization of this fact brings him to stillness. He has touched upon a truth, a discovery within, a moment of "know thyself." That moment is eternal. Whatever any living being has uttered at that moment of stillness is part of eternity.

The mind that has freed itself from all illusions and deceptions comes to stillness. It then discovers that any words it utters that are of ideas have no meaning. They're false. Ideas have no validity. Truth is something totally different. Truth is uttered by a state of being. Any person who is regulated by ideas — and most of us are — his life is unstable and unfulfilled.

In the world today there is a great deal of education — universities everywhere. And we have affluence. But look at the consequences. Never has man been so exhausted upon this planet. We have burned our nervous energy with more and more wanting, more ideas and clashes, more frictions, duality, conflict, frustrations. And the planet itself is tired. Worn out.

Even the seeds are losing their vitality. And seeds are not of time. The seed is eternal. You can save it for a thousand years and it doesn't age. But now, everything is worn out and tired.

And anyone who sells peace and incense, we're so happy with them. Then one day, the volcano erupts inside and you find yourself in anger, and the peace is gone. Peace is of another purity that is independent of ideas.

We are talking about the still mind of the one who

has seen, and really realizes, that the brain wants more and more, that it thinks it can learn. And today the difficulty is that we don't even know how to un-learn. Spontaneity is gone and innocence is gone. And the "knowing" leaves us no choice. It just goes on and on; it's so accelerated.

We must learn to step out of the momentum of tension and activity. Make some space in your life. Start simply at first. Start from the outside — although in truth there is no outside and inside. Start there. Put some time aside when you can relax yourself. Give yourself a break, for God's sake. Be well rested.

It's going to be difficult to end the projections or even to cope with them. It takes integrity and courage, tremendous wisdom and strength. It's so easy to read the newspapers. It's so easy to say, "Let me telephone so and so." It's so easy to become a do-gooder. Can you put all your projections aside, just for one hour? Get to know yourself, just for one hour? Then you'll find something within you — after you are recuperated, relaxed, and your mind is not projecting.

And if you fall asleep, sleep. Never mind the meditation. First, be kind to yourself. Don't go for the more-ness of meditation; you won't find it anyway. Be kind to yourself. Get somebody to give you a good massage, and then you can massage that person too.

We need to step out of exhaustion and the pressure of our projections. Find some time to heed the Course from a relatively still state, where you have the space. Do not be in a hurry to read the next sentence. Give enough space to not only read the words but to harness the energy of the truth behind them.

And then you will see how the Course will intensify the stillness. You can know the reality — not just the words. It will intensify that stillness and awaken Divine Faculties. Awaken you. And the awakening no longer wants to learn anymore. It's too sweet, too delicious, too energetic. Unless we awaken to this real gladness within, we will keep on searching and wanting and longing externally. But it is inside.

That which is inside is independent of ideas. It is independent of all things external because love is real and all external things are ideas. Then whatever you do is an expression of your goodness and silences another person.

You realize that your own goodness is the goodness Divine Forces give to you. You begin to realize that you are not separate. Then you never judge others who are different from you because they have some other ideas. You look upon what they are in reality, not their ideas. You never conclude, because the minute you have concluded, you have judged. The minute you have judged, you have violated. You have fallen into the trap of knowing. Retain your innocence. Innocence can listen and can heed the still small voice within. Innocence can listen and heed *A Course in Miracles*.

The Course is holy. It is sacred. Step by step it brings you to your own perfection, your own holiness. It does not make you dependent on anyone. It introduces you to self-sufficiency.

Then, whatever you do would be an extension of God. There won't be "you" in it. And it would be most joyous, affecting this planet for eternities to come. For a moment of truth has the power to vibrate on this planet forever.

And that is what *A Course in Miracles* is all about. Every single lesson brings one to that state, to the Mind of God. Every single lesson.

Obviously, there is a different way to read it, and to approach it. We have to approach it with reverence. It is not just something you do.

How would you approach it? Pick up the book abruptly — throw it here and there — read it — put on your shoes — "I've got to go"? If you do, then you are trying to fit it into your scheme of life. If you have a schedule and you want the Course to fit into it, you are not ready to fit into God's Mind. You have to see all these deceptions. Are you willing to kindly observe this?

Somewhere, I don't think that I can change, but I want to improve myself. And now I've got a set of books called *A Course in Miracles* and I read it and have some ideas. The minute I reduce it to ideas, it's no different than anything else.

Have we ever done anything else? Whether it's the Bible or the Koran or the Vedas or Vedanta, whatever, don't we reduce them to ideas?

And what I am continues. Nothing interrupts that. Somewhere we have to see that we have to die to the self.

We are talking about the approach to *A Course in Miracles*. Much depends on how we read it and I have hardly ever met anyone who knows to read. We read the words, but the words are not the thing. Words only represent something. The word "love" is not love. The word "America" means nothing in itself. Words are abstract.

Our words only have meaning at the level of unreality, the level of things we have projected. Therefore, we are not really thinking people — people who can dissolve their abstract thought. That would take some different kind of reading, some different kind of thinking, some different kind of light.

Are you approaching *A Course in Miracles* because you really want to step out of this constant preoccupation that gives you no rest? Do you really want to bring the brain to silence, to see its deceptions and illusions and bring them to an end? Can you care enough to come to a different state? Can you read it with that care or with that intensity that can come to the state of a silent mind? You have to put some kind of challenge before yourself. And we don't seem to do that.

If there is that burning need, then your relationship with the Course becomes different. But if it is just casual, then you can read it and keep on reading it. And people have read it over and over.

You could say that either *A Course in Miracles* doesn't work or you're doing something that isn't quite consistent. But for you to say that it doesn't work, you have to come to some kind of wholeness in yourself. You just can't be partial and say it doesn't work.

Generally, we leave things half-way, neither here nor there. Half milk, half water. In order to change our lifestyle, we have to come to being very much in love with what we're doing. To be very serious. This is what's lacking. When there's no seriousness, things become a ritual because the brain loves habit. It functions in terms of routine. It is lazy; it likes routine; it keeps on thinking when it shouldn't be thinking. It's not very intelligent.

In order to be free of casualness we have to give our attention to something. What is it you love, that you really care for? Where is that quality of reverence, where we don't constantly try to fit things into our routine? Each sentence of the Course is going to confront us with a challenge. But you and I don't have the time. We don't have the space. And probably, if you don't mind my saying, we don't live right. And so our energies are dissipated. Therefore, when a challenge comes, either we are going to put it off or we are going to start yawning: "Some day I'm gonna do it." That is like Hemingway saying: "Tomorrow I can do everything." It's quite a dumping ground.

Are you willing to put compromises away? Then there is urgency. Are you beginning to see what I'm saying? Urgency brings one to attention. And we cannot come to attention as long as the urgency isn't there. So we have to see what brings urgency. When the rattlesnake is right before you, you have urgency.

Why do we compromise? We cannot read the Course unless we understand what compromise is. Compromise creates opposites. That's the key.

This little story might get the point across. I come

from an Indian village where there were not very
many people who went to school. We had a school in
the village but we'd rather play than go to school.
Some parents, however, were very particular that
their child go to school. After this grade school, he
would go to the town school three or four miles
away. And then after that, to high school.

If he went to college, he would be away for three
or four years and come home during vacation time.
And he would be well dressed and so forth. Everybody in the village would look up to him. He had a
different air about him and was no longer, so to
speak, a peasant; he was more sophisticated. And he
would bring in all kinds of words of English and talk
about this thing and that thing, and we were just so
full of wonder.

He had information about things but he never
knew the thing. That's Mr. Education.

People would say, "You spent fourteen years and
you're still selfish? What did you learn?" The whole village was shocked that he still got angry, that he's selfish. They thought education was to bring you to some
purity, to some righteousness, some self-knowing.

The shock of the people. Can you see how the
innocent get shocked? Now, that's the background
for this story from the *Mahabharata*.

Once there was a king in India whose name was
Yudhishthira. This story takes place when he was a little boy. He had four brothers. And they were princes
and went to school. And Yudhishthira was very clear.
He was all-knowing, an extremely bright child. And the

teachers, they were very happy with him. Just a hint and he would understand the principle.

The wise don't go through the labor of learning, they learn the principle instantly and then discover the rest. Do you know how they discover it? They give it the space, and the truth of it unfolds in them. They don't learn externally through ideas and words. They learn through an awakening within themselves. The minute they question — "I don't know what love is; what peace is" — it becomes a prayer because the question has vitality. And the question is blessed, for now it doesn't accept the words. There is no compromise. It is your own words that deceive you. If you don't accept your words you will come to stillness and you will see something else flowering.

So, Yudhishthira did not learn through efforts, through the senses. One hint and he understood the principle, the Law. He would understand what love is, then he would see: My God, everything is created by Love. Instantly it unfolds because he has the space within him. We have a population explosion of ideas inside. Can you imagine someone who has that space, to let the whole thing unfold, the whole Glory of God? He sees the Kingdom.

So, the teachers were very happy because he could just instantly grasp it. Because he was totally present, he could come to awareness rather than to the words. Awareness knows everything, but it is not of words.

One day, the teacher was teaching him from a little book, and the book said, "You must never get angry and you must never tell a lie." This book is like the Indian primer, the first and second grade book. "You must never get angry and you must never tell a lie.''

The next day his teacher started giving him the next lesson, and this very brilliant being wouldn't read any further. He became tongue-tied. He couldn't go any further. So, they said, maybe he has a tummy-ache or something.

And the next day, the next week, it went on. He was stuck. His parents got worried. Teachers got worried. Students got worried. "What's happened to him?''

Finally, the teacher wanted to really shake him up. ''Come on, now. Everybody's passing you by. What's the matter with you?'' And the teacher got so mad, he slapped him. "Come on! Over a month of this? Just one line. Why can't you learn? What's happened to you?''

Yudhishthira said, "I have learned one thing: you have slapped me and I am not angry. But I still tell lies.'' And he wouldn't go any further.

Are you going to read the Course that way? Are you going to read the Course that way — without knowing what compromise is?

A Course in Miracles brings action into your life to end ideas, and to discover your own holiness that does not compromise. It brings one to a state of being that is untouched by compromise.

If you're satisfied with your kind of non-reading, it's up to you. If there's urgency in your life and you're serious, then we have something to do. Learn what it is not to compromise. Otherwise we know a lot of words and they don't mean a thing.

A very nice woman recently spoke with me. She said, "I have studied these books six years and I still get angry. Today I was weeping. I can't learn it. I can understand it and then I can't fully learn it. I can't become it. I can't become what I'm supposed to become, through the book. I understand how He's teaching, how the mind is operating, or rather, how the human ego is operating, but even though I can understand it, I can't. . . ."

In a way that's everyone's dilemma, isn't it? So we begin to see that one person's question is everyone's question. We're all in the same boat. And we see that compromise gets the better of us, prevents it. And compromise is there when urgency is not. We need urgency because urgency brings us to seriousness, to being very attentive.

If that is what we are interested in, then we have a wonderful foundation from which to begin. If you want to come to seriousness, then you see that compromise does not lead us anywhere — in six years, sixty years, or six thousand years.

It's like Carl Sandburg said, "There's only one man in the world, his name is all Men. There's only one woman in the world, her name is all Women. There's only one child in the world, its name is all Children." We are all dealing with the same brain that loves to compromise and loves to postpone, that has its illusions and is caught in its knowing that does not know. And in order to break these bonds, we have to come to a state that is non-compromising.

And that is our difficulty. We are too comfortable; we can afford to compromise.

If the brain can put it off, that's what it will do. It has invented a tomorrow and it will read it the seventh time. It can do everything but stop its chatter or question.

What we are talking about is seriousness. Unless one is serious, one will never step out of the brain's preoccupation. And we have been content with our answers. If we can't find the answers then we find a guru who gives us an answer that pacifies us. This is what a compromise is.

When you can't pacify yourself with your own conclusions, you'll get somebody else's. Someone who is cleverer at it. But that is not religious, because religion is a state of being. It is innocent and silent, and it requires the understanding of why we compromise. We have to start from seeing the fact that our life is a series of compromises. Real religion would make us very miserable. Can you see that we are children of compromises; that that is what we have reduced ourselves to?

We are afraid of crisis and we want to play it safe. We must see the fact as the fact: that we compromise and religion has nothing to do with compromises.

But don't condemn yourself. Just be the witness and observe. And then you'll see that we don't want to look at ourselves. We always want to deviate into something else. Can we be honest and just observe? Start with knowing yourself. How do you kill time? Where does your energy go? Find out whether you really want a religious life that is a state and not a dogma. ''Know thyself'' is the beginning of wisdom. And that's all we need to know. Put your idealism away. Get to know yourself — your motivations, your consistencies and inconsistencies. And don't cover it up. Justifications are never valid. Observe. Don't be afraid and don't blame or condemn. Just observe.

You and I have to learn one other thing — something called reverence. This is very alien to the West although the Orient doesn't have a monopoly on it. Without reverence we will not come to silence. This is very important. Reverence is neither Oriental nor Occidental, Christian nor non-Christian. It doesn't fit into anything. Reverence is a quality. It is like a gentleness.

You know when you love someone, how gentle you are? Have you ever noticed that? When you love someone, you are gentle and you are kind. And that gentleness brings about an atmosphere where each person then opens up to give. You are thoughtful and your touch speaks. The caring civilizes you. You create an atmosphere where something much deeper can be shared. It's something very beautiful. And different.

That is reverence for life, respect for another, love for your own self. Because reverence is where you want to give. Without reverence you want to take. Most sexual relationships are where you want to take, release tension, using and abusing bodies. And that is not it.

When I first touched the Course, it imparted something to me that is the most precious thing I have ever known. More precious than my own life. Because without it, I didn't have a life. And therefore, I have reverence.

If I was crossing a river while carrying the books, I could not let the water touch them. And when I travel, I have them in a little carrying bag, never do I lose sight of it. Never do I give it to another nor put it on the floor.

For me *A Course in Miracles* is the Thoughts of God. And it civilizes me. It lifts me. To have a relationship that is lofty demands the purity of myself. And I can't throw it around or treat it as if it were just words. If you do, you don't have a relationship with it.

When I read it, I hear God speak. It is not words then; it is something else. It leads me to the truth of the lesson, the wisdom of the lesson, the energy of the lesson. It is extraordinary. To see one day, *My meaningless thoughts are showing me a meaningless world*[17] — and to discover it — frees you from all the world's commotion and plans. You are untouched by them. You can be in the world but not of the world.

Change your relationship with the daily lesson.

Sit quietly, give space, come to gratefulness and reverence so that you can receive. It has Thoughts of God to offer. And we need to approach it with reverence.

Religion as a whole, throughout the ages, has put a lot of emphasis on concentrating. Concentration means negation of everything else. In itself, it's isolating. So, concentration is not it. You become self-centered and further separate yourself. Can we see the mischief of organized religions that promote separation?

There is a difference between attention and concentration. When you are relaxed, not concentrating, more aware, you read the Course as if not even pronouncing the words because you have the space. So, the emphasis is not on words, but on what the words communicate.

Every word then becomes a law. And the depth of every line is a revelation. It takes one beyond understanding. It takes one beyond discovery. It takes one beyond realization. It takes one to the actual state of recognition. And you recognize that you are not separate anymore. It dissolves the separation. Every single lesson. Every single reading.

What a blessing to live according to the curriculum of *A Course in Miracles*, the curriculum of God, for a year. But do it with reverence and give it the space. When you are hurried, you can't fit it into your life. *You* have to change. And change is the most difficult thing in life.

That's why the real teacher has very few students. He insists upon changing and they insist upon learning. And there is no relationship between the two.

A Course in Miracles is to be lived. Otherwise, it's like everything else we do — a preoccupation.

There have been a lot of scriptures and they are all holy. But none ever brought us, step by step, to application. They talked about Moses and Jesus, Rama, and so forth. But one does not know where to begin. And here it is, finally, something given that has a step by step, evolving process.

And are we just going to read it and not bring it to application? What does it impart? Do you receive the benediction of the lesson? Do you see what the difficulties are in bringing it to application? How far does understanding go? Is there such a thing in life as understanding? Do not take anything for granted.

You can go and teach the Course like hundreds, maybe thousands, are doing. But to really know what the Course is, the truth of it, is a different matter. It has to go beyond your interpretation. You can use the Course to make a livelihood and also think you're helping people. As long as there is that illusion, is it ethical? Is it ethical? The Course is not something one sets out to teach. That's going to require some ethic. One must bring it to application.

In other scriptures we never had the key to bring to application what Moses said or Nanak said or Rama said or Jesus said. We were told how good it was but nothing was given in order to bring it to application. I mean in a systematic way. But the Course has the basic, inherent vitality and benediction to bring us to application. That's what makes it the Gift of God.

The thirty-fourth lesson is: *I could see peace instead of this.*[18] We all do want to see peace, don't we? And what prevents it? We don't even know what peace is. That's a hard thing for us to accept, that we don't know. But it would revolutionize our life if we were honest. How? For the simple reason that if we knew what peace was, we couldn't settle for anything else. In peace there are no alternatives. It is so beautiful, so complete, whole. Peace makes everything else secondary and trivial.

In that state, you see everything else is an illusion and you can't become a part of it. You can't be involved anymore. You have trust in the Divine order of existence. And therefore, manmade fears and rules and conditionings, likes and dislikes, everything that is of duality ends. And we find it difficult to admit that we don't know it.

What constitutes peace? What would be its action? Obviously, its action would be independent of our personality. It would be an Action of Creation. There is only one Reality — the Creative Action of Life. The plants extend it. Birds in flight manifest it. The waves of the sea, the movement of planets — all an extension of the same Creative Force. And there is no danger of one from the other because there is no other in it.

So *I could see peace instead of this* means that we see peace, or we see Reality, and not what our thought is projecting. Don't we always see what our thought is projecting? It's probably the only seeing we've ever known because we think with thought and we see with thought. We look through thought.

By the time Lesson 34 comes in *A Course in Miracles* we have seen *My meaningless thoughts are showing me a meaningless world.*[19] We have already gone through the challenge of *My thoughts do not mean anything.*[20] That disillusionment, that outgrowing has already taken place. And if it hasn't, then we have not read it rightly, or we have not given it the reverence, the attention, the space that is needed.

Somehow, doesn't it enliven one to know that I have never known peace? I have known gratifying sensations; when I was happy there was pleasure. Those moments I have known, but I have never known peace — an understanding that is beyond the words, not touched by thought. It would have to be beyond words, otherwise our thought would take over very quickly by putting some worry into it, some anxiety into it. Thought would take care alright. There wouldn't be any peace left, even if we ever blundered into it.

When I have read the lesson, *I could see peace instead of this,* it means that I can let go of everything else. And if I can't let go, then I'd rather see that instead of peace. Some action, some decision, some transformation must take place. But we don't allow that to take place. And therefore, we stop short of peace. It remains a word. Politicians, they play with that word. But the word is never the state, never the actuality. What about the actual? Why is it we don't want peace?

We make it some kind of a learning. What a deceptive word! I wonder if we ever learned anything? Such an illusion, this thing called "learning." It must have an end somewhere. What a liberation to be free of it. We need to come to the end of learning in order to know peace.

Peace is not of thought and is not of personality. The personality somehow must stay out of it, but we can't seem to let go. So, the personality wants peace and prepares for war — armament, the whole national politics, economics — everything inconsistent with it.

And somehow, the great miracle of the Course comes into our hands and says you have to find it within yourself. The externals are not going to give it

— not the commercial, not the religious, not the polit-ical. Anyone who is somewhat aware and objective sees the degeneration. Things are out of control, out of hand, everywhere in the world.

Affluence is the poorest state of being. No one has his own water. There is separation in everything, not even natural clothing. No morality. No ethics. No eternal words in a man's life that circumstances can-not affect.

Look at the crime, the drugs. Observe the family situation, every individual life. And *A Course in Mira-cles* says you can have peace instead of this. We don't know what that means. We live a life of such stimula-tion. Night is not night. Twilight is not twilight. It's go, go, go. No pause in our life to step out of the momentum and hold hands with God.

Begin to see the poverty and tension of it, the acceleration of it. Where does the human energy go? The human, God-given energy? Corporations are rich. And we are so oblivious. Every single thing has contradicted itself.

When men like Jefferson were working on the Constitution, it was something new to the world, a great gift. They called it Democracy. How far we have gone astray. We have gone totally contrary to what was set before us. At that time, you voted for some-one that you knew. You knew about his ethics, the moral principles by which he lived. And today you vote for a person you've never met or even known. How do they earn all the money they need to run for office? What are they going to do? Their own conflict makes them incapable of peace. And you think they're going to bring us to it? Some kind of right-eousness has to be there — in life.

So, in the midst of the degeneration comes *A Course in Miracles* which gives us a daily lesson that says: You could see peace instead of this external torment and illusion, a world of unreality where you are helpless and there's nothing you can do.

And the Prince of Peace offers His Hand and says:

> *If it helps you, think of me holding your hand and leading you. And I assure you this will be no idle fantasy.*[21]

Have you a moment to hold hands? When you hold hands with Him, you step out of time into eternity. And you would never return to time again. For you are responsible by the time you have read the thirty-fourth lesson.

Then you have one function — to bring all involvements and all loose ends to an end. You make right use of time; your life becomes productive. And you never solve problems with the overdoing of wrong. You are thoughtful, you are loving, you are not impatient. You have brought about a transformation in your life that is related with everyone else because we exist in relationship. Now there is goodness and kindness.

Right away, there is a change in you. And you're not going to do anything inconsistent. You would see the Action of Creation that is ever perfect, helping you to end your involvements and your obligations. And you would say, "My God, I was never aware of the Action of Grace!"

You would be so pleased inside; that in everything, the Universe helps me to bring the false to an end. What is it? The Prodigal Son comes home. For you are looking at the world's unreality differently. And when you are at peace, that is how you will see it — differently. You don't quarrel with it. You don't become a reformer, make a cause, interfere in other people's lives. We can hardly take care of our own.

But we think insecurity is more important than God and disobedience to Divine Principles is better than rightness. There is another approach to Life.

And now we can talk about the word "approach." What do you think it is? We're going to read *A Course in Miracles* and so everything has to change. We have to know the fact and the reality of the word "approach." We have to go beyond the dictionary meanings. We have to undo everything to know what approach is. And here we walk around thinking we know when we don't. Do we know what it means, the approach?

Well, let us see what approach means. When I approach the thirty-fourth lesson, I can do it as if it is a duty to read it and then put it away and get on with what I have to do. The momentum of "me and mine" never seems to cease. Do you see? I'm going to fit the Course in here, do that, and go. Aren't I? Are you being honest with yourself when you're reading it? If you already have plans, you don't think the miracle is going to take place in your life. You don't think the thirty-fourth lesson is going to change you or you couldn't possibly have another plan about what you're going to do after you're finished.

Have you ever read it that way? Without the plan? Where you go to read the Course and you have no plan that you're going to do this and you're going to do that. Because you don't know what *it* is going to do. If you do have a plan, then you're not going to be reading the Course.

Is your interest in bringing the self to an end, the "me and mine" to an end? Have you ever approached it in a different way? What must that approach be? That the minute you pick up the lesson, that you do not project anything as to what's going to take place. Then you'd read it differently, wouldn't you?

I would like to use two stories to clarify this.

There was a great prophet named Nanak. Extraordinary being. He was in India but he travelled a lot. He went all the way from Assam and Burma, all the way to Mecca. And he was always freeing people from their belief system. The prophet has nothing to teach. He just frees you from your deception. That's the work of a prophet, isn't it? He's not the one who gives you another belief system. Beliefs are a bondage.

Nanak would question people. And he would always be doing things that were inconsistent with the belief systems, with the rituals. Therefore, he would get into trouble. But in reality other people got into trouble because he asked them some fundamental questions. "What do you mean by approach?" he would ask. Oh God, they never bargained for that.

If he went to Mecca, he would sleep with his feet facing Mecca. And oh, the Moslems would die for such an insult. Even if he is on another continent, a

Moslem makes sure which way Mecca is before he sleeps. You know, for the head must be facing Mecca.

So Nanak does the opposite, and they tell him, "Move your legs." They might think he's blind or old, or whatever. But he started showing them who was blind when he said that God was everywhere, not only in Mecca.

"Is there a place that He is not?" he asked. Simple question.

We have to question everything in our own life.

One time, Nanak encountered a priest, and the priest said, "I want you to meditate with me." Nanak was available, that's his job. He would loosen people up from their knowing. He represents the Unknown, the unbounded Glory of God. He's a messenger of Love and Light, a man at peace who has outgrown words and manmade concepts.

"So be it," he said, and sat down. The priest did a lot of praying and then finally sat down to meditate. Well, after some time passed, the priest got up and said thank you. And Nanak said, "What do you mean, thank you? Did you meditate? You're all the time worried about the colt falling into the pit."

The priest had a colt and while he was meditating he was thinking, "Oh God, I forgot to tie him up. He's going to fall in that pit. I should have told my son."

"You're worrying about the colt falling into the pit. I thought we were going to meditate."

Are you going to read *A Course in Miracles* without bringing something to an end? Otherwise, it's not a reading at all. And the old continues.

Do you have that reverence for the Course? Would you like it to bring you to a miracle with each lesson, that ends the past and brings you to peace and to timelessness, to the truth of your being? A different approach, isn't it?

What is our approach to reading a lesson of *A Course in Miracles*? Half measures? A duty? A ritual? A repetition? Then, we can read the whole book without having read the first lesson. And I wonder if whatever we do isn't just the same. That if we do that with the Course, we do that with everything else. Half measures and half-truths. Can you tell me one thing you do that you're totally present with? A different approach.

Let us say there are two approaches. There is one approach that continues the old, that continues the "me and mine", that continues the past. And there is another approach that ends it, that brings one to newness.

A Course in Miracles is meant, each day, to end the old approach — of ritual, of half-truth, of not being present. Now, let us see what that really means. The personality has one approach with its errands and its activity of self-survival: the pursuit of safety, of security, of pleasure — whatever you'd like to call it — you know, this thing that goes on and on. That's one approach. It could be called the approach of motives, ever moving towards self-advantage.

And in that world, we are sold all kinds of skills and all kinds of panaceas, all kinds of religious phraseology, one thing after another to improve us. Zen, democracy, economic freedom, communism, enterprise, you name it. They're all for sale, aren't they? Medical systems, history — dead past digging graves.

So there's one, the approach of half-truths and partial actions. We will call that "activity" and we will call the other approach "action." Action is of Life and activity is of personality. If our approach is of personality, it moves toward self-advantage and it engenders fear, selfishness, self-centeredness, all kinds of illusions and separation. And we never step into the newness of peace.

The other approach is something akin to a prayer. Prayer is not words. It is an action that precedes thought — some other action that takes place before the prayer.

But we go to thought in order to pray, and *thought* says, "Oh Lord, . . ." in the way we're trained and skilled. You know, you may as well go for a bicycle ride. It's not a prayer. It's a ritual.

And we settle for that. "I prayed." We're never going to admit that it hasn't worked. We'd have to face some challenges, wouldn't we? "I didn't pray right," or "I'm a hypocrite," or "Why can't I pray?" We don't want to come to those crises.

Then we pray again — tomorrow. But, if it isn't doing anything, then somewhere one must question that maybe it's the wrong approach.

I'll tell you what the thirty-fourth lesson means. We used the story of Nanak and the priest. Nanak had said, "Sit down there. You didn't meditate. You were worried about the colt. Your brain was preoccupied." And so this priest would have gone on so-called meditating without ever knowing what meditation is. So why do we lie to ourselves? Where is the energy to question falsehood, our helplessness, hypocrisy? That would be a religious action, wouldn't it? An action of Life that we can't live without.

Another story I'd like to share is also consistent with the thirty-fourth lesson.

There was a priest in India, and there was a little temple that he used to take care of. He was a professional priest. You know — good with meek words and all that. You'd never know what furnace went on inside, but outwardly — professional.

There were some images of gods in the temple and it was a Hindu custom that the priest prepare the food, and before he would eat, he would take the tray and put it before the idols. So, he would do that. He'd close his eyes, pray, offer the food to the gods, bring the tray back and eat it. The food is blessed, he fed the gods and he fed himself. Everything was OK. (There never is a system in the world that does not work things to its own favor. Every business policy, every political policy, every religious rule — all are to their own advantage. Isn't that so? Open your eyes and see.)

Now, one day something happened to his son who was some distance away. The priest was in crisis. He had to go. He had to go and he can't not feed the gods. You understand? That ritual. And he didn't know what to do.

So he looked around and there was this simpleton — a peasant boy who never saw a book, couldn't read, couldn't write. His name was Dhana. He saw this boy in the field and said, ''Look, I've got to go. My son. . . . I have to go. Now listen you. Wash yourself. Take a bath. Quick. Then you prepare some food and feed the gods. This time you feed the gods.''

Well, the boy is so scared. He feels so clumsy, so out of place, so crude. Dhana is scared stiff. He never thought himself worthy to even go to the temple.

Now the priest is in a hurry, in crisis, so he can't explain too much. So he says here's this, do that, so forth. ''Don't tell me you can't do it. I've got to go.'' And he left.

So Dhana took a bath. Then he cooked some food. And all the time he's feeling very inadequate. He's shivering. Anyhow, he prepared the meal and took it to the gods in the temple, rang the bell, closed his eyes, said his prayer ''Ram-Ram'' — whatever it is — opened his eyes and the food is still there.

He said, ''I'm good for nothing. Please, please have mercy. Eat the food. He'll be back tomorrow, but just take this now.'' You know, it's so nice to be innocent.

The food is still there. And he pleaded. He prayed a little more. More *slowly* this time. Food is still there. He says, ''Oh God, I'm so crude.''

So he comes back and he prepares another meal,

now with much greater care. And he's praying all the time. All that he knows he's putting into it. Clumsy thing, men don't cook in India. But here he's got the job. So he prepares it and then he goes back.

He says to himself, "It's late. They must be hungry." So he put it there and sat down and really prayed. Opens the eyes and the food is still there.

And he says, "God, now please. It's not so tasty but it's late and you must be hungry and I can't cope." But the food is still there.

Then he begins to see that he's crude. He wished he was sensitive. He wished he could cook. He wished he could do all kinds of things. Then he bows down with his forehead on the floor and he's really praying as hard as he can. "He will be back. He told me he will be back. Just one meal." And he looked and the food was still there.

Now he doesn't know what to do. He doesn't know what to do. So he went and got the kitchen knife. And he said, "I can't live if I am this bad that you won't accept my food. I can't live."

For him, the future had ended. He had no other plans but to get that food eaten by the gods. They had a priest for a change! And he took the knife and he said, "Either you're going to eat that food or I'm going to kill myself."

And the food disappeared.

Dhana became a saint in an instant for his tomorrows had finished. He had come to a new approach

— that of wholeheartedness. He put his whole being into it and he discovered that wholeheartedness is religious.

When you ask yourself a question, will you or will you not approach your computer brain for an answer? If you don't, then there are words that are not of the computer brain. So, the approach then is never to be deceived by one's own knowing but be willing to receive that what is Given to give.

Each seed produces what it is, doesn't it? When you receive what is Given to give — look at the beauty of it — you are never limited. Your resources are boundless. You cannot calculate anymore. All the resources of Heaven and the universe are yours to give because you have learned to receive to Give.

And you discover what He meant by ''Love ye one another.'' You discover love is the only thing you and I can share. There is no other sharing in the world but the sharing of love. And it inspires you. ''My God, I thought there were many kinds of sharings.''

In reality, the only thing God shares is Love. And that is all you and I can share, love with one another. And nothing can touch it. Nothing can frighten it. Nothing can buy it. When a man has love to give, he's of Heaven. He is rich. It doesn't need education. If he has it, alright. But nothing else is necessary.

Dhana never had education. He just took it literally that the gods needed to eat. It's so beautiful to be innocent. We're too clever. None of us could be Dhana anymore. He just didn't know. The priest said, ''Feed the gods.'' And he took it for granted. He came to wholeness, and they had to eat it.

So, there is an approach called wholeheartedness. If you don't have wholeheartedness to offer in order to receive the miracles of the lesson, the truth of the lesson, then it's only a ritual. But if you're wholehearted, to wholeheartedness is given the glory of that lesson. Wholeheartedness will receive the peace.

Be wholehearted about the lesson. I don't know what else we could be wholehearted about that has peace to impart instead of the problems and the preoccupations that we are caught in. Anxiety, pressure, on and on, activity. We need to be liberated from ourselves.

Peace liberates man from his own bondage. And bondage can never be improved by political systems, or economic systems, or organized religions.

We have known the partial actions in our life and now we have the Thoughts of God offered by *A Course in Miracles*. Could we please be wholehearted? For the only function of man upon this earth is to discover his own identity — that he is timeless. We are extensions of God. And we are not to hold anyone's so-called wrong or right against them. We are to love one another.

Because love is real and our ideas about wrong and right are false, we are offered the system of the Thought of God to outgrow the manmade thought system. Man's system of thought is based on self-centeredness and on separation. "I must look after myself; I must improve myself." And the Thought system of God says: We are all an extension of One Life and we can see peace instead of separation.

But we need to change the approach. We need to come to reverence and read it by being totally there. And the gift we would receive will be a gift that is already given to us. And we would be most grateful just to know that it's always been there and that we have been absent.

The approach that brings the absent back to his own identity is the approach of wholeheartedness. Whatever it does is an extension of rightness. And rightness can never be affected by anything external. It brings about a change within a person. You have integrity and you have conviction because you are with rightness. And nothing external — neither atom bombs, nor earthquakes, nor economic depressions, nor unemployments, nor recessions — can touch a person who is with rightness.

A Course in Miracles is given to man at a time when we have become so dependent; when mankind and his militarism, his politics and commercialization have gone berserk. You can see that. Could we turn from the external to the internal action of God within?

I could see peace instead of this.

Peace is inherent and anxiety is manufactured by us. It's not of God. Love is of God, but we can't afford it. We have gone to hate and to fear and to wars. There is hardly any hope in society. These are strong words. But there is hope in the individual.

And we have to take that responsibility — each person. Wherever you are, it's possible. Whoever you are, it's possible. It is possible because whoever you are is no longer real once you get to this. Comparisons end and the ''me and mine'' finishes. When you are at peace, that is what you give to your neighbors, to your child, to your wife, to your husband. The peace that is within you — not the peace one talks about.

When you have it, the trees know it, and the land you walk upon knows it. You affect the entire atmosphere of the planet with your peace. One man changes everything in creation. One Jesus, who can say, ''I have overcome the world,''[22] offers His hand to each and every one to overcome the world.

And every single lesson offers it. How can you and I not read it with reverence or give it the space? You don't have to be dependent on anyone. Your daily lesson is your daily bread — your daily bread of Truth. At peace, you are endangered by nothing external.

And in this feverish world of panic and fear and pressures, you can hold someone's hand too. You have the space to give the person, to listen to their problems. All problems are born out of helplessness, and they're just illusions. They're not real. And you can tell the person, ''We can cope with it. I am with you.'' Where two gather in His name, Heaven is between the two.

We have not yet known the power and the glory of peace. Man could never turn to armament, or to cheating, or to falseness, if he were at peace. It brings simplicity into one's life; it uproots all that is unessential. It has space and freedom from time. And the approach is different.

Each day, you eagerly go to the lesson. You have observed how it unfolds in you, its gladness, a song of joy. You sit quietly. And wherever you sit, it becomes holy. Immediately you make the room neat. You begin to see, "My goodness, I don't need this. . ." It's just like the mind — crowded! You want to get rid of things. And you just don't throw them out. You see who needs them. Everything you are going to do will be born out of rightness because you're not pressured anymore. It is the action of care and love.

So, simplicity comes in and with it, the Light of Heaven in your life. And you sit quietly, at peace. The very room changes. Everything is blessed by the peace of God, by the peace of man. When you read then, there is no haste and no hurry. Every single word introduces you to wholeness — to the truth of it.

A Course in Miracles is not words. It is a state of being that has outgrown the words and is with the peace it speaks of. Inherent in it is the blessing to bring us to that State. It is the greatest gift. Approach it with love and reverence. Give it your whole heart.

3

Living And Teaching
A Course In Miracles

There is a very lovely prayer in *A Course in Miracles* that begins:

Into Christ's Presence will we enter now. . .

Christ refers to a state of being, not the man Jesus. Within each person is the Christ State if they want to get to it. Jesus was one person who demonstrated the Christ State.

> *Into Christ's Presence will we enter now, serenely unaware of everything except His shining face and perfect Love. The vision of His face will stay with you, but there will be an instant which transcends all vision, even this, the holiest. This you will never teach, for you attained it not through learning.*[23]

See how beautiful it is.

. . . for you attained it not through learning.

* * * * *

A Course in Miracles cannot be taught; it can only be shared. And we should explore what the difference is. When someone lectures, they lecture on a subject they have learned. It's always information *about* something. They can talk about the Roman Empire or about the bottom of the sea and the kind of fish that live there. Things like that. And that's about all we have known for the most part: the lecture that is about something. It can be very interesting, too, but if you didn't hear it, it wouldn't make any real difference. Lectures have not changed man. We have had a lot of lectures. Every day in the universities, colleges, schools, lectures are going on. But man continues going towards the mundane — drugs, violence, and so forth.

Sharing, on the other hand, is different. It is demanding. It requires attention. It is not an accumulative process. Please be aware that we have only known the accumulative process. We gather information. It could be about Shakespeare, geology, geography — anything. It's accumulative. Then we think we are very erudite, learned. And if someone else has spent more years listening to lectures and reading books, then we think that person is ahead of us or even better than we are.

But greed is greed and anger is anger and fear is fear. And these remain within each person whether they are educated or not.

And one could ask, "What is the difference between lecturing and sharing?" Sharing is not accumulative. Sharing is not a one way thing. It is you and I that share. And if we share something eternal, then I call it real sharing. Giving my views and opinions about something is not it. How limited we are when we cannot go beyond our own or someone else's opinions.

If we do not know the unknown, then what are we going to share? Just our opinions or what we have learned from another? Are we getting the idea?

We said that sharing demands attention. What do you think attention is? What does attention mean? In reality?

Please begin to see how little we know about anything. And yet there is no end to our opinions. When we come upon something basic, something eternal, then we are silenced. Don't you see? And it becomes a bit embarrassing. So we like to be in an environment where we are not challenged, where nothing is demanded of us.

The human being is an expert at avoiding challenge. He stays at the same plane. You know, the fashions change — clothes, hair, neckties — but essentially we don't want any kind of a challenge where the accumulative process is threatened. Isn't that so?

Regardless of the society in which we grow up, we automatically accumulate its prejudices, opinions, and views. The Italian remains an Italian, the American remains an American, and so on. It is in this way young people are indoctrinated with particular beliefs.

And then comes industrialization. It says: whatever your belief is, that's your business, but to make a living you had better learn this and that and so forth. So somewhere the Hindu, the Moslem, the

American, the Russian, become the same. Are you beginning to see?

And the driving force behind it all is still just accumulation. Accumulation must be very enticing.

What is at the core of wanting to accumulate? Self-improvement.

At this point, we won't go into whether we really improve or not. But the fact remains that we like to accumulate and therefore lecturers and the opinions of other people are very popular.

When we are not fully attentive, only the process of accumulation is present. And when we are not fully attentive, we settle for the partial. But when we share, there is attention; and the energy of attention is that of awareness. Awareness is the only thing one can share. And where there is awareness, there is a Divine Presence.

When one person out of millions shares rather than lectures, then there is a Presence. Divine Presence. Then he shares his awareness. That is why it can be shared.

So the one who lectures looks down on people saying you know less and he knows more. We like that. It makes us feel very safe and doesn't make any demand.

Awareness brings something of another dimension to the three dimensional human being. Only when man comes to stillness can he know something else called awareness.

Awareness is no longer interested in information about things. Awareness is not only of this world of physicality, the manifest world; it is of the Source behind the world. In awareness there is wholeness. In awareness is totality. Awareness is not caught in or limited to time or space. Awareness is of One Life, One God.

If we don't give the space and the attention, we can't come to awareness. And therefore we deny ourselves. Then when we meet scholars and religious people, we think they know. But they are mere interpreters, talking about something they learned from another. It is not real, not their direct discovery.

What you can accumulate is never real. Why? Because when you accumulate you're not free. Freedom is in awareness; and awareness is not interested in accumulating. And in that freedom, you learn what the daily lesson of the Course is, the reality of it. The lesson of the day imparts its blessing if you are attentive. And this is the gift of the Thoughts of God, *A Course in Miracles*.

Make space in your life — some space where there is no intrusion, where you are at peace and at stillness. And then read the lesson so that you can communicate with that which is eternal. The Course, when it is read that way, is your communication with a light being. The only thing you can do is give it the attention. Once you give it the attention, then the brain is still. And you have received the gift.

So you ask, "What is the definition of attention?" Attention is not intruded upon by thought, therefore it flowers into awareness and awareness is impersonal. It's the first time the little baby that has grown to be fifty has learned to let go of fear and the accumulative process. Then you've outgrown all lectures and everything else, for you have found what you were looking for within yourself.

So, the function of a real teacher is to be a challenge. There's nothing to teach, don't you see? As long as there is insecurity, we can't even learn — we just accumulate words. Insecurity won't learn. Fear won't learn.

Can you imagine what an emancipation it would be to be free of them? How differently we would look at the world when there is no fear and no insecurity.

And I sympathize with you, because it's everyone's dilemma. Those who are insecure are often very clever. They're so intelligent in the ways of the world. It is very difficult to bring them to innocence and gratefulness. Very difficult. But it is possible to be free of it.

So we say, the real function of the teacher is to confront. Now, don't agree with it or disagree with it. Try to take it a little further.

What does the teacher confront? "What is this negativity of his? Why is he so mad? Doesn't he like me? I don't want that kind of a teacher. I want one who tells me how nice I am and gives me a lollypop. And the next day, hands me another one. Different color."

And we would be very happy. We'd all be doing readings and everything else. Talking about our inner teacher. Good God! Everything is for sale.

These are the things that the real teacher confronts. He confronts them because he truly knows who you are. And while you think you need a guide, you need a teacher, you need some method, he says no, no, no. Isn't that confronting? That's a big challenge. We don't want to go near such a person. And yet we all say we want to change. One who teaches you — who preaches to you — certainly underestimates you.

The teacher has got to challenge because he knows that you're perfect. But the one who doesn't know anything about perfection says, "Look, now, I'm going to give you a method." Doesn't he? Don't we all go for that? Haven't we done that all our life? Every hour projecting something?

We are always projecting and then pursuing those projections. Who's free of projections and images?

Unless we really see that this is what we do we cannot put an end to it. What kind of challenge you have to be to yourself! That's quite a lot of work, isn't it?

So, as long as we live by the values of our own projections — which means, of our own knowings — nothing really gets across. Why doesn't each one of us see: "My God, what resistance I have!" That would be a miracle, wouldn't it?

What I'm trying to communicate is first that the teacher has to be a challenge. Jesus was. Mr. Krishnamurti was. I'm sure Buddha was. And *A Course in Miracles* is a challenge too.

So, the teacher must challenge. And he only chal-

lenges because he has seen that any kind of means of
arriving at it is false — that to first project something
and then want to be there cannot work. Would you
not give him some thanks? Maybe it took centuries
and centuries to discover this one pearl. There are no
means to it. There is no doing to it, to arrive there. It's
not from here to there. There is no there. Because
there is no tomorrow. Here is a person who says:
"My God, mankind has been lost in this!"

And the preachers and the gurus sell you tomorrow, don't they? Do this, this, this and then you'll get
that. You went to schools. That's how they trained
you. What have you known that wasn't that way? So
then, your own knowledge is going to defeat you,
isn't it?

In ancient times, wise people were very, very
selective. They only shared with that person who
could really contain it, who would not abuse it, who
would not commercialize it or draw attention to himself. Then the student himself came to a freedom. He
realized the truth and was finished. He was a light.

But we are so indoctrinated to accumulate
knowledge. Why? Partly because we think we're
nothing. And indeed we are nothing as long as we
are not related to the reality of who we are.

The real is only God and His Will and His extension. Nothing else matters. All human beings then
are one and the same, aren't they? So status doesn't
matter. But where there is insecurity, we think he's
great, or she's great because she has written a few
books or something. But if you've outgrown all
things, you say, "My goodness. This is of a meaning-

less world with its meaningless thoughts.''

So, the teacher is the one who challenges. He challenges because he knows the perfection that you are. He challenges in order to introduce you to your perfection rather than to put an extra coat of paint on you.

And we don't like that. We say: ''Leave me alone! I don't want you to take my projections away. What are you doing to me? How am I going to live? How am I going to make a living?'' You know, somewhere the fear is not going to let go of us.

The real teacher must know the perfection that God created in you — not as an idea, but as a truth. Do you understand? And we don't know what truth is because in truth there are no two. Get it? Ah! Otherwise, it's just an idea. Anyone can say, ''In truth we are all one.'' But unless it's realized, it's a lie! Isn't it? Don't buy anybody's lies. But lies sell. Like hotcakes.

The teacher sees that you're as God created you — that you are perfect — and he introduces you to your perfection. Tell me in what way can he do it other than by challenging your belief systems? Would he not have to do so?

And then he says: ''Alright. Now you've learned from me that you have to challenge. You are perfect. You have the resources. You can do what I have done. And so now, go your way. Now you can help others.''

He doesn't make anybody dependent.

And now relationship — which we have never known — comes into being. Before we only knew dependence. So the teacher gives the birth that even the parents didn't give. And he deals only with those people who are ripe. That is why he never becomes a public figure. He has no ideas to sell. He can only deal with a few.

You have no idea in the ancient times what reverence they had for that kind of teacher. Not the teachers that were teaching you mathematics and geography and so forth. The real teachers were so different. And they did simple things — simple things.

In my early twenties, I spent four years in the Himalayas with meditations and such things. And when the anniversary of the birth of a great prophet came, many traveled to his birthplace to pay homage. And so, I went too, with a group. We were all very serious, really serious.

We didn't tell lies, we didn't look at girls, we did the rosary. And we read the scriptures and we were good people. Sometimes we laughed. Most of the time we were very prayerful.

So we were all in one place, you know, five or six of us. And life was very simple. I don't remember ever carrying anything. Isn't that nice? Perhaps just a shawl. Too hot, put it down; too cold, drape it around. It was so simple. And everything was provided. It's a different culture.

Now we're going to introduce you to a saint, a very beautiful person. One morning we got up very early, because this was the day of the anniversary.

You know, a real Christmas Day. And the idea is to go very early. Things start at 2:00 or 4:00 A.M. And your status is according to how early you get up.

And so we got up good and early. We want everybody to know. Listen, status isn't only acquiring money and having a big house. The poorest man can find status. The ego can find status in all kinds of things. So, we didn't have anything but the nice big status, and the ego too — all draped in spirituality.

"Let's ask the saint if he wants to go to the temple with us."

"That's a good idea." (At least the saint will know we're serious. Up early.)

So we went. And very gently. It's always a little difficult to approach these people — they have a kind of aura about them, a certain kind of dignity. And a lot of ideas don't quite materialize when it comes to who's going to go and do it.

Well, anyhow, we were together, and togetherness gives one some kind of strength. And if you're young, you have a bit of that daring. The young are never courageous. The young are daring. There's a vast difference between being daring and being courageous.

We were daring. We didn't know what courage was. Not yet.

This saint was living in a little hut. He was just staying there. He didn't own anything. We all knew of him.

So we went, and we opened the door. And we

A GIFT FOR ALL MANKIND

saw the saint was sitting. And there was really such a
quiet. So we said, ''Saintji, we are going to the temple to bow. Would you like to come?''

There was no answer. And we waited. And we
waited. And we waited. There was no answer. But
we were so frozen still. And then he said, ''I went to
the temple and bowed my head once and I have
never raised it since.''

It's another light, isn't it? He ends all words, all
the ritual. Some confronting! You could write a thousand page book. The man says there are no means to
it. It is ended in him. The knowings, the searchings.

So the real teachers, they have unique ways.
Unique ways.

In studying *A Course in Miracles*, can we approach
the lesson of the day with that spirit? Can we go to
the lesson and end all thought? The lesson has the vitality and the blessing inherent in it to bring us to
that. The lesson frees us from all seeking, all of our
so-called knowing. And therefore, we never fall back
into the daily routine. Can we stay with that? Each
day we will receive the boon. Each lesson becomes
such a blessing, such a joy, and offers happiness we
have never known before. Once we have known that
joy within, we will not go for pleasure or for loss and
gain. It is when we are empty, then we seek what is
external. It's a kind of curiosity.

So, now we come back to the real teacher — the
teacher who challenges all the deceptions, all the
assumptions, all the knowings, all the conclusions,
all the resistances. And he is not going to be a favorite
with those who are not really earnest.

76

Instead of getting put off or being resistant, why not discover the truth of what he is saying. Then the truth would impart its joy. Every challenge has enormous happiness to impart. It is not a threat, it is a joy. If you have resistance to what he says it becomes a challenge. If we don't have resistance then it is a boon. Now you have your own barometer: "Am I resisting or am I joyous?" A challenge is only a challenge where there is resistance. Isn't that beautiful?

I wish that we could share the joy of a challenge — the truth that it imparts. Because love and truth become one.

Jesus said, "Love ye one another."[24] Twenty centuries have gone by. How many people do you think ever heard it or brought it into application? Something as flowery as "love?" Nobody is against it — whether he is religious or not. But who has ever honored: "Love ye one another?" What about our motives? They won't let us love another. What about our choices, our knowing and our preferences? They won't let us. But what if one really knew love?

So we can be very grateful that now we won't get taken over by somebody just preaching something and saying, "Tomorrow you are going to get it."

Would you confront yourself and challenge your conclusions? When you free yourself from conclusions, how joyous you are going to be! We have deprived ourselves of that happiness, of that light. In what better words can I express that to challenge deceptions, to challenge assumptions, is a very joyous undertaking? It is the only thing that is religious. Happiness comes into being because truth is happy.

77

Do you know the difference between God's Thought and man's thoughts? God's Thought challenges man's thought and dissolves it. That's the difference. God's Thought is the only teacher. It challenges man's thoughts and dissolves them. Then what remains is God's Thoughts.

Did you know that God's first Thought is what continues to manifest creation? Don't read it with a lot of imagination. God had a thought and that thought became manifested in the external. That thought still continues to vibrate and continues to create. You and I, our entity, came with that same thought, with the same thought that keeps on manifesting and being the co-creator. That thought is ever within us. But we have never heard our real thoughts.

Within us is the thought that has vitality but we don't want to hear it. It keeps on manifesting, keeps on creating. We are the Thought of God and as human beings, as His children, we can know what that is. Without knowing that, we will never know what truth is or what love is or what creativity is or what security is. All our false knowledge — man's thought, so to speak — is the block. And we either have fear of letting go or we have resistance. But the teacher says, "In the challenging of it is the joy because joy only comes when we are free."

I will not value what is valueless.[25]

If you burn within, you will put an end to the nonessential and value that which is essential. I think the most essential thing in one's life is silence. Can we go into what silence is in actuality — not just as a word?

We think that if we became quiet, it's silence. But you must come to silence without desire and wanting; otherwise, it is not silence. Do you see?

You say, "I'm going to be silent." And then if you don't get high, you'll be disappointed. And if you get high, you won't even be sure whether it's your own projections or not. We don't have much control over our feelings. The Course says most of us don't even know when we are happy and when we are sad. Can you imagine that we don't even have that discrimination! Most people don't know. Most of us like torment.

So somebody may not get very high, but they'll get high telling everybody else what happened to them: "my inner teacher" or "this light and that light." Just leave that part alone.

Start to come toward simplicity, toward discrimination, toward stepping out of the stimulation. That would be the right thing to do. And that's not wanting anything.

Then, you see that which has no meaning; that you do this and that because you are unhappy and lonely and bored. So you get to know how much the loneliness and the boredom rules you. Ninety percent of the shops are sustained by the loneliness of people. You already have too many clothes, too many shoes, too many everything.

Come to that kind of wisdom, to weed out the unrealities, the unessentials. Then you would have space you wouldn't know what to do with. You would learn that you need the unessentials bad or you're going to sink or die. You're getting to know yourself. At least you're being honest.

Get to know how much loneliness rules us. Where there is loneliness, it has a sister called fear. They hold hands and dance. The two put together have total control over us — over our eyes and ears, everything. They control. Loneliness and fear.

That is what rules the external world that is manmade. As long as we're preoccupied with that, we will not be related to the God created world. And we need to come to the God created world. That requires wisdom and simplicity and discrimination.

The Course tells us that what changes is manmade. What does not change is of God. It's not of time, for it is eternal.

We can learn through our own wisdom. And then you will discover what you really need is in God's hands. And you leave it there.

Make some space. Sit quietly, in silence, and certain kinds of things take place, if one observes. First, how long will it take for one to come to silence? The brain would still be going on and on.

But stay with it; don't be impatient. Don't say, "The brain doesn't leave me alone," and activate it all the more. Just leave it alone. Be it so. Because the function of the brain is to bring all illusions, all confusions, all contradictions, to attention.

But now our minds are only the conscious mind and it is trained. Are you there? Only one part of ourselves, what we call the practical self, is highly trained. And then we are scared stiff of any other part of ourselves.

Some time ago, a child wasn't pressured to go to school so early. He developed a kind of harmony and therefore, wasn't overly conditioned by the externals. He still had something of his own, his own music of childhood, own discovery, own stillness. Now it's shattered. ''Go to school.'' Or, ''Watch the TV.'' And it's getting worse and worse and worse. We are being crippled.

And therefore before we go to bed, we don't have the time to bring all the unfinished business of the day to attention so that it can be dissolved. The loose ends — unfinished this and that — can be brought to attention. You can make a note, ''I have to write this letter. I have to do this.'' Then the brain would come to stillness because it has nothing more to report. When we are busy, only one part of our brain is very active.

When we sit still, we awaken the other parts of the brain. As it comes closer and closer to wholeness, more and more quiet, the gaps between the thoughts begin to widen. That's the sign of relaxation.

Did you know that all thoughts have a gap in between? When you're angry, they get shorter. When you hate somebody, there hardly is any gap at all.

By sitting quiet, the first thing it would do is widen these gaps between the thoughts. This is a natural process. As it begins to widen these gaps, another energy comes into being.

This other energy is called mutation. Mutation is something that has its own light, that takes place in the brain. It may not happen the first day or it could happen right away. But stay with it.

Staying with it is to master your habits and impulses and urges. When you sit down, you're going to find things that you need to do that you never thought of before because you never gave yourself the space. "The dishes need to be done. Oh, I forgot to call so and so. Ah, I didn't get the laundry."

Don't be agitated by it. Let the brain do its reporting. A day will come when the brain will report all that needs to be done in the first five minutes and you'll be grateful.

Then you will learn never to take on anything that you're not going to see through. You won't write a letter that's unessential. You won't use words that are sentimental lies. You become a responsible person.

And you would see the gaps between the thoughts widening and you'd feel a peace. And those wider gaps bring one to the present. You will become as if a witness to what is happening. But you will never get involved.

As these gaps begin to widen, new cells come into being. And they get energized by silence. Otherwise, you're burning that same energy with thoughts about this and that and so forth. And it's exactly the same energy.

The gaps are timeless. They come when you're relaxed, when your thought is not all that active.

Through these gaps come certain clear moments that are far swifter than thought. You could have been thinking about some things for two days or two years and in one split second, they become clear. Because the gaps are of wisdom.

These gaps eventually begin to silence the thought. First they widen; you have the energy; and then they begin to dissolve the thoughts. And you think, ''My God, how could I have been such a fool? They seem so superficial, these meaningless thoughts.'' They begin to drop away.

And then, as more of the space becomes clear, then you see this mutation taking place, that you come to light. It's an energy within the person. This light is the light that doesn't see with physical eyes. It's the light of eternity. It's the light of all creation, created by vibration and light.

But we, the physical, only see the gross, the dense: rocks and trees, you and me. Or, it has abstract ideas: I like it, I don't like it; this is good, this is not good.

But this light sees that which is of God. It is holy. It is a light untouched by time, not limited to space. A few moments of this light is worth all of one's life. You feel as if you have lived, that you have seen the glory. It dispels the bondage in which you were caught.

You are then the Son of God, extending the Light of Heaven. He does not live by manmade rules or his fears, boredoms, or opinions. He's never concerned with survival. It doesn't even enter his head. All is perfect. Everything is holy.

And you would never become a guru or anything like that. The issue of status doesn't arise. And you'll never look down upon another human being because you'll see the other as God created him, radiant with his holiness. You realize that he can't see his holiness because the gaps have closed so much and he lives in stimulation, doing things he should not be doing but finding justifications for doing them. You begin to see how he is caught in his own self-projected littleness.

And then read the Course. You make your decision that you are the child of God and your yearning will bring you to that clarity and to that light. Don't let anything interrupt that. And if you get interrupted, don't ever blame yourself. It's alright. Start again.

Never have a negative thought. It's negative thoughts about yourself or about another that prevent that clarity. They're like dark clouds within us. We grope in the darkness that we have created. And the fears and darkness are not real. One moment of that light and they are all gone, dispelled.

We are here to extend Heaven. We need a body to do so. But now we are so immersed in the body — trapped in it. And we think nothing else is real. But there is the Mind. The Mind is independent of thought. The Mind is independent of the brain.

Our physical entity has a brain and its function is to look after itself. The brain only sees separation because I'm dedicated to my preservation and you're dedicated to your preservation. If you're hungry, I can't feel your hunger. The pang of it. If you're thirsty, I can't feel your thirst. My brain can't feel your pain. Each body has its own limitation.

It is the thought that man projects and learns from another that keeps him so worried about tomorrow and its insecurity and survival. All these things are just ideas and we've gotten taken over by them.

We are not just the body. In this other silence, there is another clarity. That clarity is the clarity of the Mind of God. We are part of the Mind of God. We are part of the Will of God. In the Will of God and in the Mind of God there is no separation. That's the only state that knows what Love is. Love is eternal. It is not of thought. It is a reality. Peace is eternal. It is a fact and a truth. They are not of time.

So as we sit silent, that clarity brings us in touch with the Mind of God, and nothing is outside of it.

One such person changes the vibrations of the whole planet. You can feel the presence of such a being miles away. He need say nothing.

It's not a doing. The person who comes to this stillness has a blessing to impart. But it has nothing to do with the brain. Just his presence is a blessing. He doesn't have projects. Just his being is enough. He's always with the Word of God. He gives Voice to the Word of God.

And the Word of God is always love, always true. It's never caught in outside religious forms and behavior patterns, dogmas and theories. It has nothing to do with it. Nothing to preach. Nothing to sell. It just sees the other as holy as he is himself. It sees that there is no other reality than: *I am sustained by the Love of God.*[26]

Stillness is content every moment and renewed by the Love of God, by the Light of Creation, the Source of Life. And it has no wanting in it.

Make space in your life so there is space between the thoughts. So that we are touched by His grace. Perhaps you could set aside a little place in your house — some small corner that's beautiful, simple. There is no need to buy too many things. Find a place where you can go and sit quietly. Put a few flowers there if you like. But somewhere where you hold hands with God.

You can get some pictures of people. But the pictures should be of people who are in an exalted state. Then they are not just pictures or photographs, they are of that state. Therefore, you're never looking at the personality. It could be Jesus or Buddha; it could be anyone or any thing for that matter. Beauty can bring your mind to stillness.

You will see how a gladness will begin to flower within. Think of God; talk of God; make His Name real. You see, the memory of His Name is already within us. It has been protected throughout the ages. Your sitting quiet brings it more and more to your attention. And then you'll find that He's not outside, and He's not a Name. He just is.

Don't think you are a wicked sinner or a lowly worm. Forget about it. That's just extending your opinions of yourself.

Love has no opposite. God can't change His Mind because It's beyond all changes. That which is non-changing and ever sacred is within us.

And the world needs that. We need peace. When you have it, it would surround you. Isn't that nice? You don't have to go anywhere, learn this and that. Start with yourself. Bring a change of lifestyle. Value virtue.

In ancient times, the early Greeks, the early Chinese, the early Hebrews, the early Hindus, had something very simple to teach. They had learned that virtue brings happiness. So that's what they taught. A virtuous life brings happiness. And today, we don't know the difference between happiness and pleasure. Pleasure is for sale.

So much wrong has been done by all this affluence and accumulation. Virtue is gone. Ethics are gone. Nothing has any meaning. We have this tremendous craving for pleasure, pleasure, stimulation, pleasure.

We're not even wise enough to know that virtue leads to happiness. And happiness is something we find within ourselves. It's not with what you buy outside. Once you're happy, you have a discrimination right away. You don't go for the false.

So, come to a virtuous life. Help somebody. Why should there be babysitters in this country when there are so many older people that are bored and lonely? Like Mother Teresa said, there are people so lonely in America, they wish they could die.

Why can't they babysit? Why can't you babysit for somebody's child? The child would bring joy into your life. It's never only the parent's child. A child is everyone's child. It's your child too. He may turn out to be a genius and help unborn generations. Let's give them affection.

So find children in the neighborhood. Call the mothers and parents and say, "If you need a babysitter, I'll be very glad. He could come to my place, or I could come there."

Make your life one of service to another person. There would be healing in your hands if you did not commercialize it, but met a need directly. When you really feel for another, that is your prayer. You would awaken within you the powers of healing, just with your feeling — that you really care for a moment.

When the two of you become one, the healing takes place. That means you really care. And that's real prayer. Love is the prayer. It's effective right then. Wanting to pray and mutter a lot of words is not it. God is not deaf.

There is a lesson in *A Course in Miracles* that says:

This holy instant would I give to You.
Be You in charge. For I would follow You,
Certain that Your direction gives me peace.[27]

It's the last prayer in the *Workbook for Students*. So, before you do anything, make sure it is consistent with His Will. And It would give you the strength and the integrity to not do what is not consistent.

You and I have to come to some discrimination where we do not compromise. "I cannot do it. It is not of God. I cannot do it." You don't have to make any declaration to another. Just within yourself. That's the voice of strength. You are somebody, and you represent Heaven.

Never, ever believe that you're helpless. Never is man ever helpless. Don't ever believe any idea that you are. You are not. It's when we compromise that we confirm helplessness.

Live for something that's real so that you never have any bad feelings about yourself. God is with the one who loves and is virtuous, therefore, not regulated by anything external. Live by the fact that *Nothing real can be threatened. Nothing unreal exists.*[28] It would become your prayer. And the silence and the mutation would free you from that which is unreal. And you would see the light has been within you all the time. It's so beautiful to know, *I am sustained by the Love of God.*[29]

There are a few things that we can do to start in the morning. Start very slowly, you know, maybe wake up a little bit earlier. Start the day in a gentle, loving way. Give yourself the space, because the body has the energy then.

And don't get too busy with the errands. They are unending and they'll go on, even when we're not here. Be very loving to yourself. Rest well, eat well, don't put yourself in the second place. Insist upon right food.

So, get up slowly in the morning and be at peace with yourself. Give thanks for a new beginning. Prepare yourself to approach *A Course in Miracles*. Wash yourself; be alert; you're going to receive the Thoughts of God. The Course is not just any words. We have to put our words away in order to heed its words.

Sit quiet. Make the body still so that your mind

can become still. Try to get to a posture in which you can sit comfortably without moving around for a long period of time. And spine straight — that's the only condition. You may want to start with leaning at first, but then gradually you would see as you sit longer that once your spine is straight you won't get tired. It would cure many, many, many diseases because the flow of other energies takes place when the spine is erect. So, that's very necessary.

Then sit quiet for a while and just invoke the Presence. The *Text* says, *I am in charge of the process of atonement.*[30] The author of the Course is intimated to be Christ — Jesus Christ. And He is . . . *in charge of the process of atonement*. Atonement means ending the separation. He ends the separation. And so there is someone who gave us this, the gift of the Thoughts of God.

Then read the lesson of the Course. Read it with all the love in your heart. Come to that spirit. And if the Course asks a question, try to answer the question. Don't ignore it. If you don't know the answer — which most probably we wouldn't — be still and it will be given to you. It is *A Course in Miracles*. If we can wait, without our own words, it will be given to us.

Every single day, the lesson sets a different vibration and brings the transformation about without efforts. We just have to be true to it. And when we repeat the lesson every half hour or every hour, it reminds us that there is a God, that we are eternal and not subject just to the pressures of time. And you can welcome that. Just for a moment. It doesn't take long. Just for a moment. And that becomes a prayer. Prayer is never the words that you utter. Prayer is the intent, that which precedes the prayer. And you bring something of light into your life.

Discover how beautiful you are, how holy you are. Wherever you walk, there is a blessing that you take with you. Man brings the blessing of Heaven to earth. Be at peace; find time to be quiet; give yourself the space, and spread your wings for you are not of the earth.

This should not be difficult because you are giving yourself the gift and you are not dependent on anyone. By just discovering who you are, you will see the beauty in another. You will relate with the holiness in the other, the eternity of the other. And in eternity, there is truly no other. There is only one life in which everything is related to something else. And in it there is no fear, no insecurity, no tomorrows. It is a blissful, alive, energetic present.

Put away the fear of loss and gain. Have a garage sale and sell most of the junk in your house. Simplicity offers one space. There is great wisdom in simplicity. Buy what is healthy and natural and learn conservation. Put away wastage. We are too wasteful.

Be simple. Fall in love with yourself and silence. If you want to read something read that which is virtuous, not sensational. Read the Sermon on the Mount. Put your heart into it. Scriptures are Thoughts of God. It is the quality of reading that makes the difference, how present you are with it.

Read Emerson and Thoreau and don't go near newspapers. They just excite more and more war and conflict. But superior to all reading is your own quiet. Then out of that quiet you can say: *To everyone I offer quietness.*[31] Pray for the world from your heart. In your words. *To everyone I offer peace of mind.*[32] You have to have the peace of mind to offer. Make sure. Otherwise you are lying to yourself.

What can you offer if you don't have it? But your desire, your eagerness to offer would introduce you to it also. *To everyone I offer gentleness.*[33] Be gentle. Learn the peace and the goodness of gentleness. Be different. Be yourself.

Also pray for good will and peace. Pray for all peoples of all nations. Drop the idea that somebody is wrong and somebody is right. There is no enemy where there is love. Don't ever look upon another person that they are of this clan, this race, this political or economic system. There is no such thing. We are all human beings.

Some of us have to step out of the collective insanity. Pray for the heads of the governments — that they will make decisions that are consistent with love, consistent with life. Your prayers and your good will will have their own effect.

Bless the whole planet, and everything that lives and shares life with you upon this planet. Send your good will; don't limit yourself. Don't pray for a few friends and stop there. "Bless me and my wife, my son and his wife, us four and no more." That's not a prayer. What are you trying to do, educate God? That's some prejudice.

Pray for everyone. And forgive people — especially those you are in disagreement with. Nothing can justify our disliking a human being who shares the same life with us. Sit quietly before you go to bed and send your love to that person, and you'll come to peace. Send your love to him so that when you go to bed, the day is closed; it's all clear. You have no animosity. And your quality of sleep would improve.

Sit quiet and relax yourself. Then read the *Text* of *A Course in Miracles*. Get closer to that which is real. Step into a state that is no longer pressured.

Sleep well. Get yourself rested and if you are too busy, relax sometime during the day. Twenty minutes is all it takes during the day and you will be with a totally different vitality. Everything ends and one is refreshed. Don't tax yourself — projecting, following, projecting, following illusions. Be kind to yourself.

Fill your heart with gratefulness. With gratefulness will flower a gladness within that you have not known. Then you have something to give to the world: your joy, your gratefulness, your gladness. And the world needs it.

We are blessed with the gifts of night and sleep, the awakening of an energetic newness within us at dawn, and all the stars in the sky. It's a very beautiful world, a world expressing God's perfection and the holiness of life. Why walk the sordid manmade world of opinions and reactions?

> *To everyone I offer quietness.*
> *To everyone I offer peace of mind.*
> *To everyone I offer gentleness.*[34]

If you are consistent with that, if you are gentle,

you will offer gentleness. When you are at peace that is what you will extend.

Take your peace everywhere you go. Thank you and God bless you.

PART II

The Challenge

I will step back and let Him lead the way.[1]

We walk to God. Pause and reflect on this. Could any way be holier, or more deserving of your effort, of your love and of your full intent? . . .

Your feet are safely set upon the road that leads the world to God. . . Forget not He has placed His hand in yours, and given you your brothers in His Trust that you are worthy of His Trust in you.[2]

There is a light in you which cannot die; whose presence is so holy that the world is sanctified because of you. All things that live bring gifts to you, and offer them in gratitude and gladness at your feet.

I walk with God in perfect holiness.[3]

*   *   *   *   *

The wise, it is said, works with what is at hand and not with what should be. He discovers the potentials within ever adequate, thus avoids dependence and remains forever untouched by insecurity. He is not a guru who lives off of other people's money. He knows his supplies are met beyond his need. And,

What He has given me is all I want.[4]

There are those who are quick to understand and very slow to bring to application. And there are those who are slow to understand, but quicker in application.

Since man is so indoctrinated with relative knowledge, the Action of Absolute Knowledge is totally ignored in the present lifestyle. It threatens the conventional. Organized religions, for the most part, merely strengthen prejudice and educational systems limit man to the relative.

Seemingly, mankind learns a great deal, yet he never changes.

There is only one action — that of Absolute Knowledge. All problems and all of man's misery are due to his adherence to relative knowledge. Problems and solutions are the conflicts within the unreality of relative knowledge.

Jesus came to state that Love is the Law whereas the external organized religions are of concepts and belief systems. Christ lives within.

Only the one who has mastered forgiveness and who lives by Eternal Laws sees the Christ in his brethren. All He states is:

". . . forgive them; for they know not what they do."[5]

The fear, insecurity and reactions of relative knowledge are all illusions. Separation is not real. People caught in the illusions of consequences want to solve their external problems. But the real teacher insists upon the correction within.

It is impossible to see two worlds.[6]

There is no in-between.

The real teacher never deviates into the relative knowledge of cause and effect. He has no vested interest. He does not live by expectations. He does not want to accomplish anything.

The Kingdom is perfectly united and perfectly protected.[7]

Student: Why is it so difficult to understand something even when seen as truth?

The Absolute is of no level; and the relative knowledge of levels caught in contradictions is forever in conflict with the truth. Ideas bind man to beliefs, and he is blinded by their illusions. Belief systems are not necessary and can be dropped instantly, for they are of one's own making.

The real teacher brings you to the awareness that he has nothing to teach. He imparts to the student the joy of gratefulness, the energy of urgency and the benediction of responsibility. His life is an expression of:

I thank my Father for His gifts to me.[8]

It is the non-separation from the Holiness of God.

It is your awareness that sees the unreality of the irrelevant. The teacher transmits the awareness, but it is not only his. It is Absolute. The Absolute is all-including, whole and holy.

In each person's life there are only three alternatives:

1) to come to the decision to end the separation and be part of what the Course calls God's Plan for Salvation. It is for those who have passion and discrimination, for those who yearn to know the God within.

2) to remain as you are, with your own status quo of abstract ideas and concepts. You have free will.

3) to be split; to want to be part of God's Plan for Salvation yet remain consistent with your own status quo. Thus, with stalemate, evade the decision. Most people fall into this category, for they validate time and postponement.

We have seen that almost everyone is convinced that they belong to the first category — but in fact, very few are earnest or can discriminate between "wanting" and "decision."

As a rule, people are not content with the situation they are in. Therefore, the lure for change is inherent in the situation, and drifting from one thing to the other is what they call change. It is a civilization caught in the activity of alternatives.

To break away from this mania is the change that

hardly anyone makes. The attraction for the opposite is ever there.

Only the wise and the mature, having seen the self-deceptions, come to the sanity that effects the change. The issue with different people may take different forms, but each one is faced with the same *decision*. The lines of demarcation are clear. We refuse to be beguiled.

It is impossible to see two worlds.

The curriculum of undoing and unlearning is what students of *A Course in Miracles* undertake to honor. But if this is worked-up enthusiasm, it wears off at the first obstacle. Discipline is deliberate and powerful, and to it, Divine Forces are added.

It is essential for us to know that the human brain is limited to body senses. Therefore, what it learns and knows does not bring one to realization of the truth. And truth is of the Mind of God we share. Thus, merely to stay at the mental level does not suffice.

In "the Course is to be lived" is implied that it requires the energy and conviction to make the breakthrough. The Course prescribes, in each lesson, the steps to take. Unless one gives the first priority to the practice of the lesson, one will not know the remembrance of God that joins your mind with the Reality that you are.

Ours is the Ministry of Gratefulness. It is our gratefulness that ushers in the action of the New Age. For, without Its energy and gladness, we will not be able to overcome the world.

God's Plan for Salvation is synonymous with Gratefulness. There is no better way to dissolve our problems than through the Holy Instant of Gratefulness. The Holy Instant is free of the binds and deceptions of personality. Gratefulness knows no crisis.

Man in isolation is pressured. The wise, timeless and swift of pace, is of the vitality of Creation, which is not personal. To be with "What Is," there is an art in keeping the personality out.

Students of the Course have undertaken to CHANGE from fear to love and to not allow the past to intrude in their lives. This is called transformation. It is revolutionary. Always spacious, always at peace, it wants nothing, for it is with its own function.

Find out where you stand. This you need to know.

Have you seen:

— the insanity of "me and mine," that it has no existence in reality?
— the deception of ideas, that they are abstract?
— the illusion of the future that is self projected?
— the bondage and perversity of individuality that is of time, personal and unreal?
— the fallacy of accomplishment, that it projects the future fear and violates the purity of trust in the Spirit that states:

I will teach with you and live with you
if you will think with me . . . ?[9]

Without faith, nothing is possible. What exactly is your relationship with the Christ Who declares, *I AM HERE?*[10]

"Who walks with me?" This question should be asked a thousand times a day, till certainty has ended doubting and established peace.[11]

A Minister of God, who walks with God in perfect holiness and lights the minds which God created one with Him, needs to know what the truth of Atonement is and live according to the Laws of Forgiveness.

Are miracles a part of your life?
Have you come to revelation?

Does the Creative Action of Life within you transform personal relationships to Holy Relationship?

Have you expanded your awareness and realized:

I am as God created me?[12]

Every hour on the hour, we have to bring to our remembrance who we are and what our function is, to bring the Course into application.

God is the Strength in which I trust.[13]

Is this your conviction?

God's Voice speaks to me all through the day.[14]

Can you say that?

I am sustained by the Love of God.[15]

How would you actualize this?

My only function is the one God gave me.[16]

Have you any other?

I am under no laws but God's.[17]

How can we avoid the realization of this?

Light and joy and peace abide in me.[18]

Are you grateful?

I thank my Father for His gifts to me.[19]

Do you?

The Minister of God must delight to extend the Will of God, knowing there is no other Will but His, that all is holy and that his brother is not separate. To realize that there is no separation in life is the joy of sanity. Without being one with the Will of God, it is not possible to heal.

As Ministers of God,

> . . . *our function is to let our minds be healed, that we may carry healing to the world, exchanging curse for blessing, pain for joy, and separation for the peace of God.*[20]

The Course states:

> *Those who are healed become the instruments of healing. . . . For here is truth bestowed, and here are all illusions brought to truth.*

Would you not offer shelter to God's Will? . . .
And can this invitation be refused?[21]

Sharing, in reality, is the vitality that sustains life. It is the free life that knows no ownership. How the world faces the challenge of mental lack is the issue.

We are aware that the resources are always in man's relationship with Heaven. Once the sharing is mastered, the religious mind of non-separation will be entrusted with the abundance of Its Spirit.

No one can fail who seeks to reach the truth.[22]

The New Age begins with the dawn of sharing. As part of God's Plan for Salvation, we are learning to share, for there are truths we learn only when we are free of insecurity.

The Course stresses that honesty is consistency at all levels of our being. We have to see things from an Eternal Perspective. Society is not apt to change, but it is still possible for the individual to come to an inner transformation.

There is the urgency for each one in God's Plan for Salvation to heed. The Course tells us that a handful of Ministers of God could change the very vibration of the planet and turn the tide.

We start with the joy of Self-giving. There is no real productivity but in Self-giving — for it is of Divine Origin. Its perspective of sanity and wisdom sees "the false as the false."

Disillusion is the first and the required step before

coming to Self-giving. Self-giving is not possible as long as there is insecurity. Disillusion is a MUST to realize one's own responsibility in finding the potentials within. The process of dependence on the externals has to be reversed so as not to rely solely on the body senses.

We have been isolated from the wholeness of our Being. The physical senses without the spiritual faculties do not relate man to the Eternal Laws behind appearances.

A Course in Miracles points out:

BY GIVING YOU LEARN TO RECEIVE

and describes the part "Love ye one another"[23] plays.

Behind appearance and behind the limitation of our thought process is the inexhaustible Source of all manifestation. We do not realize the Source of our being because thought itself stops short.

Jesus had no money.
Buddha left a kingdom.
Behold the blessing They imparted for all time to come.
Their productive life remains our treasure.
In Creation, patterns change,
but Laws remain the same.
Truth is true forever, whatever the conditions.

The boon bestowed by *A Course in Miracles* upon mankind is a dynamic action of sanctity. It is akin to the Noah's Ark.

GRACE IS WHAT MAKES IT POSSIBLE.

God created man in His own Image to bring the Kingdom of Heaven to earth. The purpose of man, who has the capacity to receive Grace, is to extend the Will of God on earth.

Grace is acceptance of the Love of God within a world of seeming hate and fear. By grace alone the hate and fear are gone. [24]

All things man does in separation from God are unreal. There is nothing to learn, nothing to undo, when he is awakened to his Reality. How unfortunate to bind our eternal holiness to the physical level.

Student: May I ask what need I do to know Grace?

Learn to forgive and put away your attack thoughts.
Never go to bed
with an unkind thought in your head.
Master forgiveness
and you have mastered the world.
You will no longer be regulated externally.

In the midst of helplessness, stay with your own conviction and the power of Love is forever yours. The joy of Self-giving will dawn in your life.

Student: But what do I do about my ignorance?

You mean — self-centeredness!
Ignorance is the illusion of separation from God.
Do not acknowledge it.
Have conviction.
Once you are firm in your decision,
the Action of Grace will end all your misperceptions
of division among men.

The issue is partial action.

If you cooperate with the Action of Grace,
it will bring you to certainty.

Student: Sir, what exactly is my problem in a nutshell?

SEPARATION.
It means isolation into personal life.
"Personal life" — this is the falsity.
But whoever heeds it
beyond the delirium of knowings?

Once you are amongst the Ministers of God, your life is no longer personal. Thus, it is protected and remains untouched by problems. You are healed by your own faith in the Action of Grace. The fact is, if you live by Eternal Laws, there is no insecurity in the timeless Present.

We all have the same problem.

Student: What is that?

As I said before, each one is bound by the physical senses' constant demand for experience. His projection of sense experiences is a difficult thing for man to give up. This is what renunciation — the final step — is all about.

Student: How do I become aware of Grace?

The moment you care for another totally, you have found your purpose that is free of all motives — natural and joyous. This instant of care is like an invocation. And miracles happen right and left. It will transform your life, for now you have something to give to humanity aching with the need for love.

There is no greater joy in life than to love another
and dispel the illusion of separation.
The discovery of the One Life,
is man's greatest benediction.

Grace is never involved.
It is with the joy of its own extension.
Just to BE, itself extends the Grace.
It is a passion yearning to give and to love,
irrespective of what another does.

Grace is at work in every life.
When we are ready to receive it,
its heavenly song is there.

Student: What is truth?

Truth is the knowledge that Love is real.
It dispels doubts and limitations.
He who knows truth, and lives by Grace,
does not commercialize his life.

God's Plan for Salvation relates with the Christ
within and joins your mind with the Reality within
you. Love, shared, is the eternal truth.

There is only one function according to the Law:

"LOVE YE ONE ANOTHER."

Student: How would I know who is a real teacher?

You have to first know who is not before you come
upon him. When this is done, illusions are no longer

your guide, and truth leads the way.

Professors and clergy the world over are inter-preters of knowledge, not men of direct knowing. The Course points out:

To let illusions walk ahead of truth is madness.[25]

The very atmosphere around the real teacher is different.

. . . where He is, there must be holiness as well as life. No attribute of His remains unshared by everything that lives.[26]

When the student outgrows the false, he gains the sensitivity to recognize and value the Absolute. Reverence for truth leads the student to discovery of the vertical teacher.

The teacher of God charges no fees.
The Holy Instant is shared.
His values are eternal.
It is the exchange of love with the student.

Student: Sir, what is a commitment?

Commitment is the inspiration of your own devo-tion that yearns to purify itself. Commitment is always to the truth. It is not imposed. Its energy puts personality in the second place. Its zest ends the authority of the past; the world of drifting and the conflict of alternatives vanish.

There is a difference between being self-convinced and having the passion that yearns for God. The man of devotion is not enticed by things of the earth.

Awareness of the wholeness that he is changes the perspective and he realizes the truth of *My single purpose offers it to me.*[27] He who walks with God in perfect holiness is the light of the world.

Student: You have said that no one has a mind of his own.

Yes. In reality, there is only the one mind — the Mind of God. The sense of ''me and mine'' separates It, but it is false. This fragmentation is not real.

Mind is your own only when it is given back to God; and it is shared, for it is indivisible.

Student: Why do I procrastinate?

Procrastination is the making of the illusion of time and self-deception. It takes wisdom, integrity and passion to come to a decision.

There is but one decision, and no in-between: truth is, or it is not!

Student: Where do I start?

With the vigilance of self-honesty.
With the love of knowing yourself.

One starts with oneself.
One starts with gratefulness.
One starts with removing self-deceptions.
One starts, not with the assumptions of wanting this and wanting that, but getting to know oneself.

We are so externalized and lonely that most of us have never met ourselves, nor have the time or the originality to know:

I am as God created me.[28]

Know the virtues of awareness. It imparts the wisdom required to be free of the pressure of time. Life is so simple, and peace so lofty. The less he has, the more spacious the wise.

We have made it complex without having the direct knowings. Yet the Creator surrounds each living being with His peace and joy. Being His children, how could it be otherwise?

Sorrow is manmade. Separation is of his own making. The truth is that we are One, and fear has no place in it.

Helplessness and anxiety are external unrealities that you do not have to accept. Undoing false identification is the action blessed by God:

No one can fail who seeks to reach the truth.[29]

Where there is Divine Leisure, there is no loneliness. The spacious Aloneness of a mystic is boundless. Every urge and impulse, wish and desire born out of frustration is for things unessential. To be false is the curse.

We are so lost and bewildered without the Compassion of God to share with another. Nothing ends the separation but Love.

Whatever we do all day, all our life — if it does not end the isolation, what good is it?

Student: I lack clear direction and peace; and my mind is conventional.

To know peace is to be productive. You must evolve within yourself to give something to the world instead of working for another.

What would you give to know how Jesus lived a single day in His life, and all that transpired in His awakened State? Five minutes with the Eternal Man is worth more than a whole life.

Value non-wastefulness and the planet will protect you. Bring order in your life so that you take no advantage of another. Then God will give you your own work to do.

Student: Sir, what is the message, or the secret of contentment?

It is only when one is not with the Will of God that one is arrogant. Out of ignorance, sorrow is born, ambition is born, distrust is born, and choices and preferences activated.

A desire-ridden life is hell and devoid of peace and joy. It runs for the sensation and pleasure of the senses that bind him to the physicality of individuality. It is all an adoration of nothing.

To be content is to be free from the known. A man devoid of innocence, simplicity and the purity of silence perpetuates his own torment.

I wish man would see the un-necessity of the hysteria of his self-centeredness and incessant need of work. If you could only allow yourself relaxation and the space just to be — free from "becoming" — you would know the potentials of Divine Leisure. Then you would learn to afford honesty and get to know what is of internal value to you, irrespective of the externals.

The joy is in the humility of a modest life, not driven by unfulfillment. When self-sufficiency blossoms, it is the most exquisite flower the world has ever seen.

> *The certain are perfectly calm,*
> *because they are not in doubt.*
> *They do not raise questions,*
> *because nothing questionable*
> *enters their mind.*[30]

It is difficult to evade the consequences of what you yourself project and set into motion. Most people are constantly actualizing their own beliefs of themselves.

The correction can only be made by the one who initiated the error. The wisdom lies in making the correction within, rather than to seek solutions to problems.

Have you not read the lesson:

> *My function here is to forgive the world*
> *For all the errors I have made?*[31]

Student: What is the deeper meaning of devotion?

Devotion is constant recollection that God is the doer. And there is no work for us to do

other than to realize that we are He.
That is devotion.

Devotion trusts the Will of God.

ALL IS ONLY GOOD.

In the absence of devotion,
we surrender our life to ignorance.

To Love, devotion is natural.
Gladness and prayers laugh and play
within its spacious silence.

Student: What is faith, and what is belief?

Faith is a direct experience.
It is something within you,
no longer subject to thought.
There is no personality in it.
How can personality know what is eternal?

Belief is changeable.
It is of transitory thoughts.
The wise never relies on it.

The Man of God does not confirm your beliefs.
He dissolves them.

Student: Sir, what are the characteristics of thought?

Being self-projected,
thought is limited to self-interest.
Anything that is of time cannot know
what is not of time.

Thought can know the past and project the future.
But in the Present,
there is no interference of thought.

See the complexities of thought itself.
Thought always thinks in terms of activity.
When there is activity, you are not present.

Thought, then, has limitation
because it is never fulfilled and always seeking.

   Student: Is it possible to be present and to be active?

Possibly it would be some creative energy
that is active
and not thought.

But see how vast is the power of thought —
that from millennia it has been with us.
Man is controlled by thought and no longer conceives
that it is possible to survive without it.

   Student: How can we stop this momentum of
thought?

That is the issue before us.
We have to know what to do about thought,
rather than disliking it.

Humanity has been steeped in self-advantage.
The educational and religious systems of the world
but strengthen the confidence of self-centeredness
to survive in opposition to God.
Man is trained in how to survive; how to make a living;
how to succeed.
This is thought's world.

At the same time,
thought does not know how to get out of it.
We are conditioned and trained
to use thought for survival.
Thought represents: how to "become."

Whenever there is "becoming" and activity,
it is of thought.
The Fact has no activity.
Could thought, then, not be called "interference"?

To cope with the projections of thought requires
urgency.
Somewhere a conviction has to come to put an end
to that which is of time, of thought.
Regeneration must begin with oneself.

　Student: If I knew how, then I could let go of
thought.

That is still the same as "becoming."
The way one thinks is always to have more thought.
We become dependent on the idea of "better wisdom."

Inherent in the thinking process is unfulfillment;
and thought maintains it
for thought is constantly unfulfilled.
This we have to discover.

The question is: is there within us a conviction
to outgrow everything that is of thought?

Simply put,
thought is the means of separation.
Awareness is the means of outgrowing thought.

Unfulfillment has been our truth.
And God's Plan for Salvation is of fulfillment.
That is Its base.

Where do we stand?
Is it postponement, or is it God's Plan for Salvation?

   Student: Sir, there is the earnest wanting within
me to take this step.

Yes, but the discrimination of WANTING versus
VALUE is most essential.

WANTING does not have the energy to break away
from selfhood, from personality.
It is of self-centeredness, ever unfulfilled.

VALUE can only be for that which is eternal.
What one VALUES
then becomes one's internal strength.

Harness the strength of the Divine Laws
and the WANTING will be outgrown.

For this, one must be tremendously attentive
not to be deceived.

   Student: What is the nature of this attention you
speak of?

Attention, which is not of the body, is of purer energy.
That attentiveness can say with conviction:

> *I am not a body. I am free.*
> *For I am still as God created me.*[32]

Passive listening knows only to turn facts
into personal opinions.
It demands vigilance and tremendous attention
to overcome our opinions.
This is the challenge.

We never realized that the delirium of our knowings
prevents us from coming to attention.
These are the impediments.

Question the learning.
Has anyone learned other than to cultivate memory?

Then it becomes a necessity
to develop the capacity to receive.
The State that knows to receive
is the State of responsibility.

And It can give to an aching world
that is so desperately in need.

Student: How can I be with the urgency of change
in my life?

Is there anything in the world of experiences
that you value more than knowing
you are a Son of God?
Find out.
Only you can do so.

Student: What is it to come to real learning?

The only responsibility is to remove deceptions.
That is the real learning.
See the power of these words.

Student: Sir, I pray to come to clarity.

Wanting the clarity is the avoidance of clarity
because clarity itself is an action into the new,
into the unknown.
It silences all things of wanting.
That is its energy.
It has something of the Spirit.

Clarity is, where the duality has ended.

The function of clarity is to introduce us to our eternity,
to the truth that we are of the Spirit.
Then will we know what it is to be productive.

Student: What is the need for *A Course in Miracles*
in mankind today?

To the degree the corporations are controlling
almost everyone and everything,
to that degree *A Course in Miracles* step by step,
is bringing one to the recognition of who one is,
so that he no longer is ruled by insanity.
A sane person is independent of all that is external
because he no longer projects.

People responsible for what they are doing
are free of consequences,
therefore, have no future.

Anyone who is moving
toward the ending of the opposite
is provided by Heaven.

Student: Is meditation necessary in God's Plan for
Salvation?

To end duality, meditation is absolutely necessary.
In meditation, the opposite comes to an end.
When you are liberated from the body senses,
then you can say,

I am as God created me.[33]

Give time to sitting quiet.
There is urgency; put your vitality into it
so that you are not subject to the externals.

It is our right intent that is blessed and provided.

Student: Sir, what is involved in writing a book?

Writing, like living, follows the Law of Creation.
He who brings heaven to earth transmits in a moment what is timeless. This newness is the light that liberates all that is in the bind of time.

What other purpose has writing?

Amen

Love does not crucify. It only saves.
God's Son cannot be hurt. Let him not think
That he is slave of time or punishment.
Created out of Love, his shining head
And loving heart can only save the world.
Who but its maker can redeem it? What
Except the Word of truth can liberate
Whom he imprisons? Let him be Himself,
And not one star can lose a single gleam,
Or flicker in uncertain galaxy
Without a purpose and without a cause.
No blade of grass but rises perfectly
From earth toward Heaven. And no sin appears
To hold in shadows whom all Heaven loves.
God does not crucify. He merely is.

This poem is from *The Gifts of God* by the scribe of *A Course in Miracles*. It is an incomparable book of poetry containing some of the most important words ever spoken.

References

PREFACE

1. *A Course in Miracles* (ACIM), *Manual for Teachers* (III), page 25.
2. ACIM, *Text* (I), page 312.
3. ACIM, I, page 313.
4. ACIM, *Workbook for Students* (II), page 18.
5. ACIM, II, page 48.
6. ACIM, II, page 239.
7. ACIM, III, page 67.
8. ACIM, III, page 68.
9. ACIM, III, page 1.
10. ACIM, III, page 5.
11. ACIM, II, page 219.
12. ACIM, I, page 6.
13. Ibid.
14. ACIM, I, page 444.
15. Refers to Matthew 13:13-17.
16. ACIM, I, page 444.
17. ACIM, III, page 8.
18. ACIM, II, page 120.
19. ACIM, II, page 107.
20. ACIM, II, page 434.
21. ACIM, II, page 233.

PART I

1. John 10:30.
2. John 14:12.
3. ACIM, II, page 79.
4. ACIM, II, page 3.
5. ACIM, II, page 4.
6. ACIM, II, page 6.
7. ACIM, II, page 16.
8. ACIM, II, page 77.
9. ACIM, II, page 79.
10. Exodus 20:13.
11. ACIM, II, page 18.
12. ACIM, II, page 119.
13. ACIM, II, page 392.
14. Ibid.
15. ACIM, II, page 406.
16. ACIM, II, page 437.
17. ACIM, II, page 18.
18. ACIM, II, page 51.
19. ACIM, II, page 18.
20. ACIM, II, page 25.
21. ACIM, II, page 119.
22. John 16:33.
23. ACIM, II, page 290.
24. John 13:34; 15:12; 15:17 . . .
25. ACIM, II, page 239.
26. ACIM, II, page 79.
27. ACIM, II, page 476.
28. ACIM, I , Introduction.
29. ACIM, II, page 79.
30. ACIM, I, page 6.
31. ACIM, II, page 192.
32. Ibid.
33. Ibid.
34. Ibid.

PART II

1. ACIM, II, page 284.
2. ACIM, II, page 285-286.
3. ACIM, II, page 287.
4. ACIM, II, page 205.
5. Luke 23:34.
6. ACIM, II, page 231.
7. ACIM, I, page 54.
8. ACIM, II, page 216.
9. ACIM, I, page 49.
10. ACIM, II, page 280.
11. ACIM, II, page 288.
12. ACIM, II, page 162.
13. ACIM, II, page 75.
14. ACIM, II, page 78.
15. ACIM, II, page 79.
16. ACIM, II, page 107.
17. ACIM, II, page 132.
18. ACIM, II, page 159.
19. ACIM, II, page 216.
20. ACIM, II, page 255-256.
21. ACIM, II, page 255.
22. ACIM, II, page 233.
23. John 13:34; 15:12; 15:17 . . .
24. ACIM, II, page 315.
25. ACIM, II, page 284.
26. ACIM, II, page 287.
27. ACIM, II, page 235.
28. ACIM, II, page 162.
29. ACIM, II, page 233.
30. ACIM, I, page 109.
31. ACIM, II, page 204.
32. ACIM, II, page 376.
33. ACIM, II, page 162.

Biography Of Tara Singh

Tara Singh is known as a teacher, author, poet and humanitarian. The early years of his life were spent in a small village in Punjab, India. From this sheltered environment his family then traveled and lived in Europe and Central America. At twenty-two, his search for Truth led him to the Himalayas where he lived for four years as an ascetic. During this period he outgrew conventional religion. He discovered that a mind conditioned by religious or secular beliefs is always limited.

In his next phase of growth he responded to the poverty of India through participation in that country's postwar industrialization and international affairs. He became an associate of Mahatma Gandhi and a close friend not only of Prime Minister Nehru but also of Eleanor Roosevelt.

It was in the 1950's, as he outgrew his involvement with political and economic systems, that Mr. Singh was inspired by his association with Mr. J. Krishnamurti and the teacher of the Dalai Lama. He discovered that mankind's problems cannot be solved externally. Subsequently, he became more and more removed from worldly affairs and devoted several years of his life to the study and practice of yoga. The discipline imparted through yoga helped make possible a three year period of silent retreat in Carmel, California, in the early 1970's.

As he emerged from the years of silence in 1976, he came into contact with *A Course in Miracles*. Its impact on him was profound. He recognized its unique contribution as a scripture and saw it as the answer to man's urgent need for direct contact with Truth. There followed a close relationship with its scribe. The Course has been the focal point of his life ever since.

Mr. Singh's love of the Course has inspired him to share it in workshops and retreats throughout the United States. He recognizes and presents the Course as Thoughts of God and correlates it with the great spiritual teachings and religions of the world.

From Easter 1983 to Easter 1984, Mr. Singh conducted the One Year Non-Commercialized Retreat: A Serious Study of *A Course in Miracles*. It was an unprecedented, in-depth exploration of the Course. No tuition was charged.

Mr. Singh continues to work closely with serious students of the Course under the sponsorship of the Foundation for Life Action — The School at *"The Branching of the Road"* to bring *A Course in Miracles* into application. He is the author of numerous books and has been featured on many videotapes in which he discusses the action of bringing one's life into order, freeing oneself from past conditioning and living the principles of the Course. He offers two regularly scheduled retreats on *A Course in Miracles* annually: New Years and Easter.

Other Materials by Tara Singh
Related To
A Course In Miracles

BOOKS

How To Raise A Child Of God
Dialogues On A Course In Miracles
The Voice That Precedes Thought
Commentaries On A Course In Miracles
"Love Holds No Grievances" — *The Ending Of Attack*
The Future Of Mankind — *The Branching Of The Road*
How To Learn From A Course In Miracles

VIDEO CASSETTE TAPES

"Give Me Your Blessing, Holy Son Of God" (Parts I & II)
"If I Defend Myself I Am Attacked" (Parts I & II)
Our Story — *What Led To The One Year*
    Non-Commercialized Retreat?
"Do Only That" — *A Course In Miracles*
    And Working With Children
"Nothing Real Can Be Threatened" —
    A Workshop On A Course In Miracles
    Part I   — *The Question and the Holy Instant*
    Part II — *The Deception of Learning*
    Part III — *Transcending the Body Senses*
    Part IV — *Awakening to Self Knowledge*
Finding Your Inner Calling
How To Raise A Child Of God
Exploring A Course In Miracles (series)
    — *What Is A Course In Miracles?*
        and *"The Certain Are Perfectly Calm"*

131

— *God Does Not Judge*
    and *Healing Relationships*
— *Man's Contemporary Issues*
    and *Life Without Consequences*
— *Principles* and *Gratefulness*
A Call To Wisdom
    and *A Call To Wisdom* — *Exploring A Course In Miracles*
Man's Struggle For Freedom From The Past
    and *"Beyond This World There Is A World I Want"*
Life For Life
    and *Moneymaking Is Inconsistent With Life Forces*

AUDIO CASSETTE TAPES

Discovering Your Life's Work
All Relationships Must End In Love
Finding Peace Within
How To Be A True Student Of A Course In Miracles
"Creation's Gentleness Is All I See"
Begin With Gratefulness
Freedom From Belief
Discovering Your Own Holiness
Psychological Pressures — *What They Are*
    And How To Deal With Them
Stories From India For Children
Discussions On A Course In Miracles
"What Is The Christ?"
Bringing A Course In Miracles Into Application
A Course In Miracles Explorations
"What Is A Course In Miracles?"
Raising A Child For The New Age
The Heart Of Forgiveness
How To Learn From A Course In Miracles (book on cassette)
The Future Of Mankind (book on cassette)
Commentaries On A Course In Miracles (book on cassette)
Tara Singh Tapes Of The One Year Non-Commercialized
    Retreat: A Serious Study Of *A Course In Miracles*

Book and tape catalogues available from Life Action Press.

Additional copies of *A Course In Miracles — A Gift For All Mankind* by Tara Singh may be obtained by sending a check, Mastercard or Visa number and expiration date to:

LIFE ACTION PRESS
902 South Burnside Avenue
Los Angeles, CA 90036
213/933-5591

Limited edition, hardbound	$12.95
Softcover	$ 7.95
(plus $2.00 shipping/handling)	

A Course In Miracles may be purchased from the Foundation for Inner Peace, P.O. Box 635, Tiburon, California 94920. It may also be purchased from Life Action Press:

Three Volume, hardbound edition	$40.00
Combined, softcover edition	$25.00
(plus $3.00 shipping/handling)	

California residents please add 6½% sales tax.
Thank you.